FAITH AND FREEDO

This Is Our Town
REVISED EDITION

Sister M. Marguerite, S.N.D., M.A.

Sister M. Bernarda, C.PP.S., PH.D.

GINN AND COMPANY
Boston • New York • Chicago • Atlanta
Dallas • Palo Alto • Toronto

ACKNOWLEDGMENTS

Grateful acknowledgment is made to the following authors and publishers for permission to use copyrighted materials:

E. P. Dutton & Co., Inc., for "The Toy Orchestra," based on the book *Joseph Haydn* by Opal Wheeler and Sybil Deucher, copyright 1936, by E. P. Dutton & Co., Inc., and used by permission of the publishers; also for "The Bread Cloud" by Lois Salk Galpern, adapted from the story in the book *Believe and Make-Believe* by Lucy Sprague Mitchell and Irma Simonton Black, copyright © 1956, by the Bank Street College of Education, and adapted by permission of E. P. Dutton & Co., Inc.

Houghton Mifflin Company for "The Fairy Book," from *A Pocketful of Posies* by Abbie Farwell Brown.

J. B. Lippincott Company for "Indian Children," from *For Days and Days by* Annette Wynne, copyright 1919-1947, by Annette Wynne, published by J. B. Lippincott Company.

Little, Brown & Company for "Grandmother Learns to Ride," adapted from "Grandmother and the Elevator" by Jean L. Couzens, from *Jack and Jill around the World* by Ada C. Rose, © The Curtis Publishing Company, 1956.

Thomas Nelson & Sons for "Apron Troubles," adapted from "How the Little Old Woman Made Her Apron Longer," from *The Little Old Woman Who Used Her Head* by Hope Newell, published by Thomas Nelson & Sons, New York.

St. Anthony Guild Press for "God's Homes" and "Within My Soul" (originally entitled "The Sacraments"), from *Poems for God's Child* by E. S., copyright 1946, St. Anthony's Guild, Paterson, N. J.

Charles Scribner's Sons for "The House without a Clock," adapted and used with the permission of Charles Scribner's Sons from "The Family Who Never Had a Clock," in *Time Was* by Hildegard Woodward, copyright 1941, Charles Scribner's Sons.

The University Publishing Company, Lincoln, Nebraska, for "Drum Music," from *Storyland* by Hazel Gertrude Kinscella.

Children's Playmate Magazine, Inc., for an adaptation of "The Buffalo Hunt" by Helen Norris Brown.

Helen Reeder Cross for "Jenny the Nightingale," adapted from "Jenny Lind and Jenny Wren," reprinted by special permission from *Jack and Jill*, © 1957, The Curtis Publishing Company.

Helen and Alf Evers for "The Wonderful Inventor," adapted from "Mr. Scrunch," from *Child Life* Magazine, copyright 1939.

Mary A. Goulding for "Francis and the Concert."

Highlights for Children, Inc., for "Questions" by Emily M. Hilsabeck, from *Children's Activities*, January, 1954, by permission of Highlights for Children, Inc., Columbus, Ohio, owner of the copyright.

Jeannette C. Nolan for "A Fine Mix-Up," adapted from "Mixed Mysteries" and for "The Lost Skates."

Ollie James Robertson for "The Wrong Side of the Bed," adapted from "Aunt Mary Molly and the Wrong Side of the Bed," reprinted by special permission from *Jack and Jill*, © 1950, The Curtis Publishing Company.

Story Parade, Inc., for "Charlie and the Whistle," from "The Boy Who Could Not Whistle" by Eleanor Clymer, copyright 1950 by Story Parade, Inc., reprinted and adapted by special permission.

FAITH AND FREEDOM

NIHIL OBSTAT:

Rev. Gerard Sloyan, s.t.l., ph.d., CENSOR DEPUTATUS

IMPRIMATUR:

†Patrick A. O'Boyle, d.d., ARCHBISHOP OF WASHINGTON

Washington, January 15, 1963

COMMISSION ON AMERICAN CITIZENSHIP
THE CATHOLIC UNIVERSITY OF AMERICA

Rt. Rev. Msgr. William J. McDonald, *President of the Commission*

Rt. Rev. Msgr. Joseph A. Gorham, *Director*

Katherine Rankin, *Editorial Consultant*

Sister Mary Lenore, o.p, *Curriculum Consultant*

PUBLISHED FOR THE CATHOLIC UNIVERSITY OF AMERICA PRESS
WASHINGTON, D.C.

Contents

■ Timber Town Today

■ Timber Town Long Ago

Getting Together Again

The Tell-a-Tale Club

Players of All Kinds

Young Citizens of Timber Town

Citizens of Heaven

Illustrations by Harry Beckhoff, Edward A. Bradford, Warren Buckley, Fred Irvin, Jack Jewell, Carl Mueller, Catherine Scholz.

Timber Town Today

Timber Town is a pretty little town. It has churches, schools, and houses. Planes from many parts of the country land at its airport.

Children and grownups work together and have good times together. Here are some stories about Timber Town today.

A Stranger in Town

"Flight C-12 is landing at Timber Town!" said a voice over the loudspeaker. We cannot land at Bear City because of the wind and rain. This flight will be grounded until three o'clock."

When the plane landed, Father Michaels got off and walked into the airport.

"Is there a Catholic church near the airport?" he asked the ticket man.

"St. Francis Church is only five streets from here," the man answered.

It was then nearly noon, but Father Michaels had not yet had breakfast. He had thought that he would offer Mass in Bear City. Now he would do it here in Timber Town.

As the priest walked away from the airport, Peter Martin and Matt Lake almost ran into him.

"Oh! We are sorry, Father," said Peter as he looked up at the priest. "We are in a big hurry," said Matt.

"What is the hurry?" asked Father Michaels with a smile.

"We just saw the new White Flyer coming into the airport," said Peter.

"Now we want to see it take off," Matt said.

"Well, don't hurry," said the priest. "It will not leave until three o'clock. I was on the White Flyer. Now I would like to offer Holy Mass here, if I can find the church."

"We'll be glad to show you where the church is, Father," said Matt.

"May we serve Mass for you, Father?" Peter asked.

"I shall be very happy to have you do that if you have time," the priest answered.

"On Saturday, we have all kinds of time," laughed Matt. "Peter and I have just learned how to serve. We like to get as many turns as we can."

"Have you ever been in Timber Town before, Father?" Peter asked.

"No, I have not," answered the priest. "I live in Watertown. Right now I am on my way to Bear City. That is, I thought I was until I landed here in your town. There is too much wind and rain around the Bear City Airport to land there."

At St. Francis Church, Father Michaels met the pastor, Father Carl. Then he offered Mass.

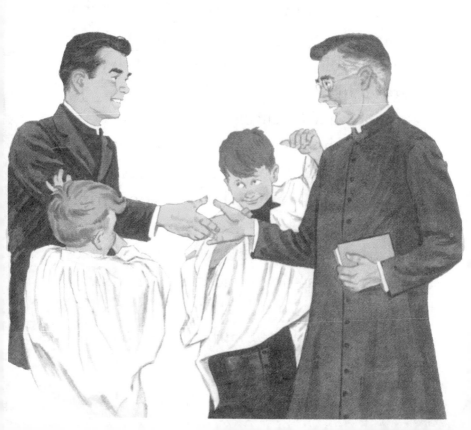

Later Father Michaels had lunch with Father Carl.

"It was nice to meet those two fine boys from your parish this morning," Father Michaels told the pastor.

"Yes, Peter Martin and Matt Lake are nice boys," said Father Carl. "We think all the boys and girls in our school are fine children.

"There is something about this town that makes the people seem different from those in other places. The grownups and children are all like one big family."

As Father Michaels walked back to the airport, he saw many people. They all seemed friendly, even to a stranger.

"Good-by, Father! Have a good trip!" someone called.

Father Michaels turned. He saw three boys running down the street. There were Peter Martin and Matt Lake again. This time they had another boy with them.

"This is Jan Cook, Father," Matt said. "He does not go to St. Francis School, but he belongs to our Space Club."

"I'm glad to meet you, Father," the dark-haired boy said with a smile.

Father Michaels liked the boys. He wanted to stay and talk with them, but it was almost three o'clock.

"Maybe we will all meet again some day," he called to the boys as he hurried to his plane.

"Happy landing, Father!" called Matt, Peter, and Jan. "Come to Timber Town again."

Space Man from Mars

"Now off for Space Station XYZ!" called Jan.

"But first we must go home and put on our new space suits," said Peter.

The boys had made space suits out of large paper bags and other things.

"We'll meet at Station XYZ dressed for our first flight to Mars," cried Matt.

Off ran the three boys, each to his own home.

When Peter got home, he took off his zipper jacket and put on his space suit. Then he looked at himself in the looking glass.

"How I would like to look like Marty!" he said. Marty was a green man from Mars that Peter had seen on TV.

Peter tried to find something to make his face green. He went into his big brother's bedroom. On the table, he saw a bottle of something green. Peter began at once to put it on his face.

Now I really look like a man from outer space," he thought.

Matt and Jan got to Space Station XYZ long before Peter did.

Space Station XYZ was a place in a field where the boys liked to play.

When the boys sat up in a tall tree, they could look down over the town. They could see boats on the river. They could see stores, houses, and churches.

They could see the flag flying over St. Francis School where Matt and Peter went. They could also see the one over River Street School where Jan went.

"To Mars!" cried Jan as the two boys climbed the tree.

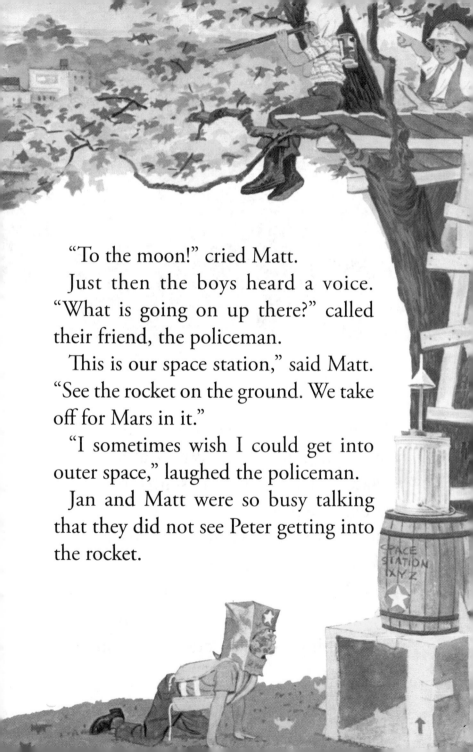

"To the moon!" cried Matt.

Just then the boys heard a voice. "What is going on up there?" called their friend, the policeman.

This is our space station," said Matt. "See the rocket on the ground. We take off for Mars in it."

"I sometimes wish I could get into outer space," laughed the policeman.

Jan and Matt were so busy talking that they did not see Peter getting into the rocket.

Later, as Matt started into the rocket, a strange green face came very near his face.

Matt turned around and started running through the field.

"Run for your life!" he cried to Jan. "It looks like a man from Mars!"

The boys did not stop running until they heard a laugh. The man from Mars was laughing as he stood just outside of the rocket.

"Oh, look, Matt," laughed Jan. "The man from Mars is only Peter in his space suit."

"Come back," Peter called. "It's your space brother."

The boys looked at Peter. He was green and looked very strange—not at all like the Peter that they knew.

"You surely frightened us!" Jan said.

"You look just like Marty from Mars," Matt laughed at last.

"Off to Mars!" cried Peter.

Then Jan and Matt, with Marty from Mars, climbed into their rocket for their trip into space.

Trouble for Peter

When Matt, Peter, and Jan heard the clock on the town hall, they knew that it was five o'clock. So they left Space Station XYZ and started home.

Peggy Martin and Melissa Lake were in the yard when Peter came home.

"Why, Peter!" cried his sister Peggy. "How funny you look! What's that on your face?"

Melissa began to laugh. "Peter, your face is green all over," she said.

"I'm Marty from Mars," laughed Peter.

The three children ran into the house. "Look at Peter," cried Melissa and Peggy in one voice.

Mrs. Martin stopped fixing dinner and turned around. "Peter!" she screamed. "What's happened to your face?"

"I painted it green," answered Peter. "I'm Marty from Mars."

"Where did you get the green paint?" his mother asked.

Before Peter could say another word, his big brother Bob called from upstairs. "Someone has been in my room and taken all of my green ink," he said.

"I think maybe I know who did it," said Mother, looking at Peter.

Poor Peter began to feel strange. He wished he were really up on Mars.

"Peter, did you take my ink?" Bob called from upstairs.

"Yes, I did," answered Peter. "I took it to make my face green."

Peter's brother came running down the stairs. "You will be sorry for doing that," he said. "That ink will not wash off. You will be Marty for a long time—maybe for the rest of your life."

Peter thought Bob was just trying to frighten him. After he had taken a bath and washed his face, he knew that the ink would not come off.

Peter rubbed and rubbed until his face hurt. Mother tried to help Peter, but spots of green ink stayed on his face.

"It will just have to wear off," said Bob, "and that may take weeks."

That night, Peter's father came home after Peter and Peggy had gone to bed. He went in to say good night to them.

When he turned on the night light in Peter's room, he could see that Peter's face did not look very clean.

"Didn't you wash your face before you got into bed, Peter?" Mr. Martin asked.

"Mother washed it, and I washed it. We almost rubbed it off," Peter said. "It's ink, and it will not come off."

"Ink!" said Mr. Martin. "How in the world did you ever get ink on your face?"

Peter's father could not help smiling when he heard what had happened.

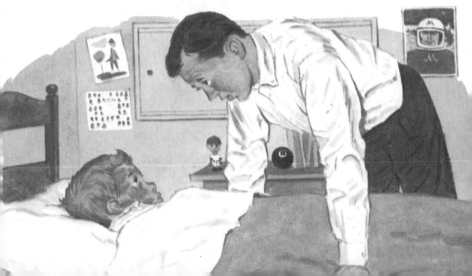

The next morning, Peter went to school
with green spots on his face.

Sister Mary was waiting for him when
he ran into the schoolyard.

"Peter," she called, "you are just the boy I
want. Father Carl needs someone to serve
Mass."

Then Sister saw Peter's face. "What's the
trouble?" she asked. "Don't you feel well?
You look very strange."

It was hard for Peter to tell Sister Mary
what had happened, but he did it just the
same.

So Matt served Mass for Father Carl that
morning.

All day, Matt tried to make his space brother feel better. He thought Peter really looked very, very funny.

"Don't feel bad about those green spots, Peter," said some of the boys. "The ink will have to wear off someday."

The next day, Mrs. Martin heard about a new kind of cream to try on Peter. She got some right away. It worked, and soon Peter looked like himself again.

"I'm glad that I am not Marty from Mars any more," said Peter. "It's nice to be a boy living right down here in this good old world of ours."

That was the last time Peter Martin ever tried to look like Marty from Mars.

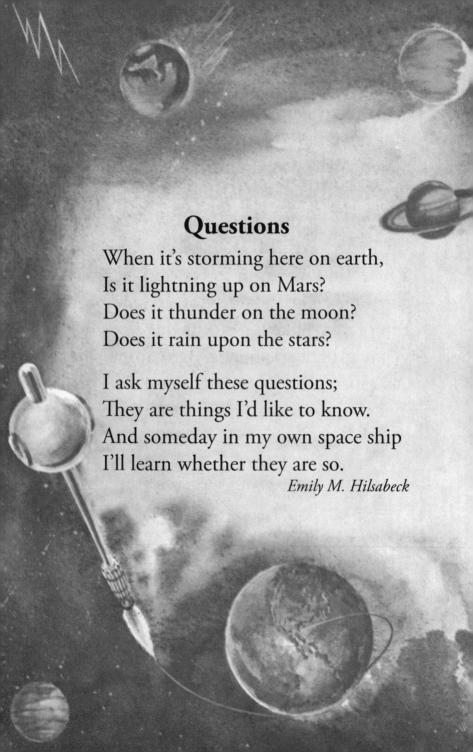

Questions

When it's storming here on earth,
Is it lightning up on Mars?
Does it thunder on the moon?
Does it rain upon the stars?

I ask myself these questions;
They are things I'd like to know.
And someday in my own space ship
I'll learn whether they are so.

Emily M. Hilsabeck

An Exciting Night

Night had come to Timber Town, and bedtime had come for boys and girls.

Maybe Jan Cook had played too hard that afternoon. As soon as he went to sleep, he began dreaming about space men. He dreamed that he was living on the moon. He dreamed that all around him were strange-looking men.

He dreamed that he heard strange sounds and saw strange things. Suddenly he heard a shrill cry that grew louder and louder. He sat up in bed.

"The space men are here!" Jan cried, before he saw that he was in his own bedroom.

The shrill cry was a loud whistle. It always let the people know when there was a fire in Timber Town.

Jan heard the whistle blow in toots. It was telling where the fire was. First there were three long toots. Then there were five short toots.

"That means the fire is on this side of the river," said Jan.

He ran to his father's room. Mr. Cook was putting on his coat.

"May I go, too, Daddy?" Jan asked.

"I guess this one time will not hurt," said Mr. Cook. "It is not very late."

The fire was in the Kings' old house on Second Street.

Many people were there. Matt Lake was there with his father. Mr. Lake was a newspaper man. He was busy writing a story for the morning paper.

Peter Martin was there with his big brother Bob.

Mr. Lake told the boys how Mr. and Mrs. King had gone away and left an iron on in their house. It had started the fire.

The firemen were working hard to put out the fire. Suddenly a loud scream came from inside the burning house.

"Help! Help! Help!" someone called.

The people looked at one another with frightened eyes. "There is someone in that burning house," they cried.

Then the voice screamed louder. "Fire, fire!" it said.

It seemed to come from upstairs in the old house. The fire chief climbed up on a ladder that was near the chimney.

"Where are you?" he called as he climbed from the ladder into the house.

"Help me!" screamed the voice.

"It must be the Kings' grandmother," said one neighbor. "I think she came to live with them just a few weeks ago."

"Poor old woman! She must be alone in that house!" said another neighbor.

"Where are you?" called the fire chief. "Be brave. We shall save you."

By this time, all the people were very excited.

"Call for an ambulance!" cried one of the firemen. "Call a doctor, too."

It was not long before the Timber Town ambulance came up the street to the Kings' house to take the poor grandmother to a hospital.

"Where in the world are you?" called the fire chief as he looked all around in the house.

Now someone was crying very loudly, "Boo-hoo! Boo-hoo! Boo-hoo!"

Down in the street, the people were talking.

"That voice is pretty loud for an old woman's voice," they said. "It sounds more like a child's cry. Do the Kings have a baby?"

"Yes, a baby boy! And he screams just like that," said the Kings' neighbor, Mrs. Muggins.

All this time, the fire chief was in the house. He looked everywhere, but he could not find the grandmother or the baby.

"Where in the world are you?" the chief called as loud as he could.

"Help, help," said the voice again.

The voice seemed to come from the other side of a door. The fire chief opened it. There was a parrot in a cage!

The chief took the cage with the parrot in it and climbed down the ladder.

All the people laughed when they saw the parrot in the cage.

Just then, Mr, and Mrs. King came up to the house in a car. Grandmother and the baby were with them.

They looked surprised to see so many people in the street. They were even more surprised when they saw what had happened to their house.

"Thank you for saving our house," Mr. King said to the fire chief.

"That's our job," said the chief. "But don't ever go away again and leave an iron on. Please take this thing, too," the chief smiled as he handed Grandmother the parrot cage.

Some of the neighbors asked the Kings to come and stay with them.

The ambulance and the doctor rode away. The fire trucks rode away, and all the people started home. It had been an exciting night.

Grandmother Learns to Ride

Mrs. Wills was a kind old lady who lived in Timber Town. She lived in a big house all by herself.

The children on Brook Street called her Grandmother. They liked to run errands for Mrs. Wills and do little jobs that were hard for her to do.

Grandmother Wills always gave little cakes and ginger cookies to the children.

One day, Grandmother Wills told her neighbors some sad news.

"I am going to move," she said. "I can't live in this big house by myself."

"Oh, where will you go?" asked a neighbor.

"I'm going to move into the new apartment house near the church," said Grandmother. "Then I can go to Mass every morning."

So one Wednesday morning, a big moving truck came and took all of Grandmother's things over to the new apartment house. Her new apartment had three rooms, but they were all the way up on the fourth floor.

On Thursday morning, Grandmother got up, put on her shawl, and went to Mass at St. Francis Church. After Mass, she prayed the Stations of the Cross. Then Grandmother started home to fix her breakfast.

In the new apartment house, there was an elevator, but Grandmother was frightened to ride in it by herself.

"It doesn't seem safe to me," she told her friends.

So Grandmother sat in a chair on the first floor and waited. She was sure that someone would come along, and she would ride upstairs with him.

Grandmother read all of the morning paper. Still no one came to take her upstairs.

"I'll walk before I ever ride in that thing by myself," thought Grandmother.

She picked up her prayer book and started upstairs. Up one flight! Up two flights! Up three flights! At last she reached the fourth floor. She was too tired to take another step. So once again, she sat down.

After a while, Grandmother started to get breakfast ready. Suddenly she remembered that she had no coffee.

"Oh, dear! Now I shall have to go all the way back down and up again," she thought.

So Grandmother put on her hat and shawl, took her pocketbook, and started to walk downstairs again.

She could have taken the elevator. It was waiting right outside her door. But the very thought of going down in the elevator all by herself frightened her.

Grandmother went to the store, got a can of coffee, and came back again. She sat down to rest before starting to climb to the fourth floor.

Suddenly the door of the elevator opened, and out came a little six-year-old boy.

"My, how brave that child is!" thought Grandmother. "He does not seem to be frightened. I wonder if I should be?"

Soon the elevator door opened again. This time Mrs. Green came out. She was older than Grandmother, and she could hardly walk.

"Well, what do you think of that?" said Grandmother to herself. "That old lady seems to like to ride in that thing. If she is not frightened, why should I be? Maybe I am being silly about this elevator."

Grandmother stepped right into the elevator and rode up to the fourth floor.

"Why, it's just wonderful the way that thing works," she told her friends. "I will never walk up steps any more."

And she didn't.

Jean L. Couzens

Kevin Learns and Earns

Kevin Cross lived in St. Francis Parish. Because his house was near the school, the Sisters asked him to run many errands for them.

Late one Tuesday afternoon, Sister Joan called Kevin.

"Will you please go on an errand for me?" she asked in a kind voice. "Mr. Long has a package for us. All you have to do is to ask for the package and bring it back."

"I'll be glad to, Sister," said Kevin, and away he went.

Mr. Long had statues, books, holy pictures, and rosaries in his store.

Kevin looked around at all the pretty things while Mr. Long got the package ready. Suddenly Kevin saw a lovely statue of Our Lady.

"How I should like to have this statue to give Mother for her birthday!" thought Kevin. "Just a few days ago, she said that she wanted a statue like this."

But, like many other children, Kevin did not have very much money of his own.

"There is only one way to get the statue," thought Kevin to himself, "and that is to take it. Mr. Long has so many statues that he will never miss this one."

Kevin did not know it, but Mr. Long could see every move he made. There was a large looking glass on the wall. As Mr. Long watched Kevin in the glass, he could almost guess what the boy was thinking.

Kevin picked up the statue and looked at it. Then he quickly put it under his coat and stood still for a minute.

Kevin thought about what he had done, and suddenly he put the statue back on the table.

"I should never have picked up that statue," he said to himself. "What must our Blessed Mother think of me? How could I ever make my mother happy by giving her a gift that I got in the wrong way?"

Kevin wished he could walk out of the store quickly without being seen. He did not want to face Mr. Long and ask for the package.

Just then Mr. Long called, "Here's your package, my boy!"

Kevin took the package and started to leave the store quickly.

"There is something more you want, isn't there?" asked Mr. Long, looking at the statue.

Kevin could feel his face grow red. He stood on one foot and then on the other.

"I should love to have that statue for my mother's birthday," he said in almost a whisper. "But I don't have enough money to buy it."

"How would you like to earn the money?" Mr. Long asked.

"Earn it?" asked Kevin in surprise. "How could I ever do that?"

"You could work here in the store on Saturdays and after school in the afternoons. You could run errands and help me in many ways," said Mr. Long.

"Could I? Could I really, Mr. Long?" asked Kevin excitedly. "How wonderful! Then my mother can have a gift that will really make her happy."

Timber Town Long Ago

A long time ago, Timber Town was just a dark forest. There were no churches, no schools, no stores. There were only Indians in the large forest until some white people came to live there.

Here are some stories about the first people who lived in Timber Town.

Father David and the Indians
An Indian Friend

A small boat came quietly down Red River toward Yohocan. In it were two white men, Father David and his helper John. They were on their way to visit people who wanted to learn about God.

"Indians!" whispered John suddenly as they came to a turn in the river. "See the Indian children. That means that there are Indians living near here."

The priest looked up and saw three Indian children playing near the water. Before he could say anything, he heard shrill cries coming through the forest.

It was too late for the priest and his helper to turn back. The Indians had seen them and were coming toward them, running through the forest.

"Let's ask Our Blessed Lord to help us," said Father David.

Together, both men whispered a prayer. Then Father David put up his hand, but that didn't stop the Indians from jumping into the river. Over they came toward the canoe.

Four of the Indians took the priest and John to the other Indians who were waiting near the forest.

It was very dark in the forest. Father David and John could hardly see where they were going, and the Indians pulled them this way and that way.

Soon the priest and his helper saw a great fire. Some of the Indian boys got up from the ground and began to dance around it.

The two poor white men were given no food that night. They were tied to two tall trees, and all they could do was watch the Indians having a feast.

As the two white men watched, they prayed for themselves and for the poor Indians, who did not know about God.

Once, when the priest looked up, he saw an Indian boy watching him. Father David smiled, but the boy only looked at the priest in a strange way.

When the Indians had finished eating, they got up and began to dance around the fire again.

After a while, everything in the forest became quiet. The Indians went to sleep.

Only one Indian had his eyes open. It was Yoho, the boy who had watched Father David praying.

Hour by hour went by. Then late in the night, something happened.

Very quietly, Yoho moved toward Father David and John. He cut the rope that was tied around their arms and feet.

"You come! The river! Be quiet!" Yoho whispered.

Slowly and quietly, Yoho, John, and the priest went through the dark forest. When they reached the river, Yoho got into the canoe with the white men.

"Are you coming with us?" Father David asked the Indian boy.

"Where you go, I go too," said Yoho.

"We are going far down the river to a village to visit some white people," Father David told Yoho.

"What will you do there?" Yoho asked.

"We are going to tell the people about God," answered the priest. "Maybe some day your people will want to learn about Him, too."

"God?" said the Indian boy. "Who is God? Take me with you. I will learn, too."

Father David and John knew that if they took Yoho, they could cause real trouble for themselves. But they took him anyway.

A Strange Surprise

Almost a week had gone by, and Yoho was still with Father David and John.

One morning at daylight, Yoho jumped up in the canoe and shouted, "White man! White man!"

"Yes," said the tired priest. "We are near the village where we will stop."

"There are some red men there, too," said John to Yoho. "They are red men like you, who want to learn about our God."

John, Yoho, and four boys from the Indian village helped to get a little house ready. The Blessed Sacrament would be put there, and Mass would be offered while the priest stayed in the village.

At noon, John began ringing a small bell. Then the people knew it was time for Mass.

Everything was so new to Yoho that he just could not keep still. John tried over and over again to tell him not to talk while Mass was going on, but poor Yoho remembered it for only a little while.

Yoho watched the people as they prayed. He heard them sing. He watched Father David change the bread and wine into the Body and Blood of Christ.

When John went up to receive the Blessed Sacrament, Yoho followed him. Father David did not see the Indian boy until he stood before him.

I'm sorry, Yoho," he whispered, "but I can't give This to you now. You must know more about the true God. Then some day you, too, can receive Holy Communion."

Yoho did not like this. He looked long and hard at Father David.

It seemed as if Yoho were going to do something when cries of Indians were heard down by the river.

Yoho's father, Chief Big Rock, and some of his people had followed the priest down the river. They had come to get Yoho and to take Father David and John away with them.

Yoho ran out of the little church.

When his father and the other Indians saw Yoho, they screamed and ran toward the church. They thought that Father David and John had taken him away from them.

Father David went on with the Mass, but he could not help wondering what might happen.

Suddenly everything became quiet. The priest thought the Indians had gone away. He turned around to give the blessing at the end of Mass.

There, at the door of the little church, he saw the Indians watching him. They did not move. After Mass, Father David walked bravely out to meet Yoho's father and the other Indians.

Chief Big Rock smiled at him. "Pretty, very pretty!" he said. "Why didn't you stay in our village and do this for us?"

Father David was almost too surprised and happy to speak.

"I'll come," he told them, "but I must stay here for a few days and finish my work."

"We'll stay, too," said Chief Big Rock. "Then you shall go back with us."

All that week, the Indians heard the priest tell about God. They saw him baptize little children, men, and women.

Father David had pictures too—pretty pictures of Our Lord and His Blessed Mother. The Indians liked the colored pictures very much. Father David gave one to Yoho and one to Chief Big Rock.

One Friday night, the missionary priest and John left the village. They went up the river with Chief Big Rock and Yoho.

The Indians did not tie John and the priest to trees with rope this time. They set food before them. They danced for them. They let them have a good sleep.

The next day and for many weeks after that, Father David told Yoho's people about the true God.

Chief Big Rock and many other Indians were baptized.

The Indians made a little church of their own in the forest. There Yoho and many other Indian children were baptized and received their First Holy Communion.

The village where all this happened was named Yohocan by all the Indians. Father David and the white people liked to call it Timber Town because of the large forest all around it.

The Buffalo Hunt

Star Flower could not sleep. The little Indian girl was very sad.

The buffalo hunt tomorrow would be the most exciting thing to happen all year. But Star Flower would not be part of it.

The buffaloes were late this year. The Indians had thought that the village would be without food for the winter.

Now at last, the buffaloes were headed toward Yohocan. The Indian scouts had come to the village to tell the news that day. Everyone was happy and excited.

Tomorrow only the old people and small children would be left in the village.

The brave Indians would go out to see how many buffaloes they could kill. The women would go to skin the buffaloes.

Boys who had been brave all year would go with the brave hunters. Girls who had worked hard would be picked to go.

Star Flower knew she would not be picked. She had worked hard all year. She had obeyed and had been good until just three days ago. Then she had done something wrong. She had played too long with some of her friends and had not done her work.

So for that one thing, she must stay in the village while all her friends rode off to the big hunt.

No one had talked to the little girl for three days. That is the Indian way of punishing children. It was much harder than being scolded.

Star Flower's kind brother Bear Moon wanted her to know that he felt sorry for her. He could not speak to her. But in the morning when she started out to get firewood, she found that some had been put near the door.

Getting firewood was a woman's work. No man ever did that. Star Flower knew that her brother must have put it there after dark when no one could see him.

On the day of the hunt, Bear Moon was up at daylight getting ready to leave the village. For the first time, he was to ride with the brave hunters.

Star Flower was happy that her brother could go on the hunt. But when she looked at his small short bow and arrows, she felt sad. She knew that he could not kill a buffalo with them. He would ride home from the hunt in a slow, sad way.

Just then Grandfather walked over and handed Bear Moon a strong bow and four long arrows. Bear Moon ran his hand over the shiny black stone at the end of the arrows. He knew that they were the arrows of his brave father, who had been killed by enemy Indians many years ago.

"Be brave! Use these arrows as your father would have," said his grandfather.

Star Flower was happy to see her brother with these strong arrows. She smiled at him as she gave him a bag of food to take with him.

"That is not enough food for two of you," Grandfather said.

Star Flower stood very still. She could hardly believe her own ears. She knew her grandfather was no longer angry.

"Bear Moon, bring a horse out for your sister," he said.

"Oh, thank you, Grandfather," Star Flower whispered. Quickly she ran to get her knife. She would need it to help skin the buffaloes that would be killed.

When the Indians started out for the hunt, Bear Moon rode with the men and boys. Star Flower felt happy as she rode in the back with some of the other girls.

There was only one more thing that she wished for. She wanted one of her brother's arrows to bring down a buffalo.

Bear Moon had killed squirrels and rabbits, but Star Flower knew that one must be very strong to kill a buffalo.

"I am happy that you ride with us," said Little Owl, who rode beside Star Flower. "It is sad you have no hunter to bring back a buffalo for you."

"My brother Bear Moon is riding with the hunters," said Star Flower proudly.

Little Owl, who was not always kind, laughed at Star Flower. "Your brother isn't strong enough to kill a buffalo," she said. "He isn't even brave."

This made Star Flower angry, and she said something she should not have said.

"My brother will kill a buffalo today," she boasted. "I am sure he will."

Star Flower should not have boasted like this. Now Little Owl would tell everyone. Then all the village would laugh at Bear Moon when he rode back without a buffalo.

By noon, the Indians came near the buffaloes. The women set up camp, and the hunters rode off after the buffaloes.

Before evening, the men had rounded up and killed many buffaloes. The women and girls sang as they skinned them.

Star Flower did not sing. Her brother had not killed a buffalo, and the village would laugh at him because of her boasting.

Suddenly a buffalo came running into camp. The big animal was followed by some hunters and by Bear Moon.

The buffalo had been hurt, and suddenly it died and fell. One of the Indian braves pulled an arrow out of the buffalo's back and held it up for all to see. The end of the arrow was made of shiny black stone. It was Bear Moon's arrow!

Bear Moon had killed a buffalo! There would be food for the winter.

Star Flower smiled at Bear Moon as they sat by the campfire that night. She was proudly thinking, "My brother is a brave hunter. He has killed a buffalo!"

It had been a happy day after all.

Helen Norris Brown

Father David Meets the Enemy
Trouble at Yohocan

Each year in the spring, Father David went back to Red River to visit Chief Big Rock, Yoho, and the other Indians of Yohocan.

He baptized babies and grownups. He gave many Indians their First Holy Communion.

One time while he was there, something very frightening happened.

It was a dark night. Not a star could be seen in the sky. There was no wind. Even the dogs were quiet. Suddenly the air was filled with loud, shrill screams.

Father David sat up in his bed of buffalo skins. "It's an enemy's cry," he shouted.

Now the Yohocan Indians were also screaming. "The Fox! The Fox are coming!" they shouted.

The Fox were enemy Indians who lived on the other side of the hills. They had come to burn the Yohocan village and to take food and horses.

Chief Big Rock gave the priest a knife. Father David did not want it. He picked up his crucifix and ran outside.

Father David cried out to the enemy and tried to make them stop fighting. His voice was strong, but with all the screaming and fighting, it could not be heard.

Then he prayed to God for help. He went about the village, trying to help those who had been hurt. He baptized many who had fallen and gave them the last blessing.

The fighting went on all night long. Wigwams were pulled down and burned. Men, women, and children were killed.

When the first signs of daylight came, Father David went out again to speak to the enemy.

"Hear me! Oh, Fox!" he cried. "I am your friend, the Blackrobe. You have asked me to come to your village. I cannot come if you do things like this."

The enemy looked at Father David and heard what he said. Slowly they began to leave and ride back over the hills.

Then Father David told Chief Big Rock that he was going to visit the Fox Indians.

"No, no!" said the chief. "They will kill you, just as they killed my people."

The priest smiled and said, "They will not kill me. They will become better people when they learn about God."

After the brave priest helped the chief set up the wigwams again, he said good-by and rode away over the hills to see the Fox Indians.

A Surprise in the Enemy's Camp

It was winter by the time Father David reached the village of the Fox Indians.

Chief Blueskin did not believe in God, but he liked the Blackrobe because he was brave. So he told the priest that he could talk to his people about the God of the white men.

On the very first afternoon, many of the Fox Indians left their wigwams to hear what the Blackrobe had to say.

Just as Father David began to speak, something happened.

A little girl ran out of one of the wigwams.
She fell at Father David's feet and cried,
"Save me! Save me! Oh, Blackrobe."

Father David could hardly believe his
eyes. The girl was a Yohocan Indian. The
Fox had taken her from Yohocan.

"She belongs to me!" screamed an old
squaw. "You can't take her from me."

"She does not belong here," said the
brave priest. "I shall take her back to her
own people."

"Then you must pay me for her," said
the squaw.

"I will give you a looking glass, some sugar, and some pretty red ribbon for the girl," the priest said.

The squaw wanted these things very much, so she let the priest have the girl.

As soon as he could, Father David took White Cloud, for that was the girl's name, to the Sisters' school which was not far from the Fox village.

"The Sisters will take good care of you, White Cloud," the priest said. "Be good, and do not try to run away. When spring comes again, I shall take you back to your own people."

White Cloud received her First Holy Communion at the Sisters' school, and she seemed very happy.

It was hard for the Sisters to part with White Cloud when Father David came to get her in the spring.

"Please don't take her away," said Sister Maria to Father David. "White Cloud is happy here. She has learned to live like white children. She will not want to leave."

Father David laughed. "Don't be so sure about that, Sister," he said. "Indians do not show their feelings. We must let White Cloud speak for herself."

Father David turned to White Cloud. "Are you happy here?" he asked.

White Cloud answered, "I am happy now because I remember the Blackrobe's promise. Now it is the moon of the birds' returning, and the Blackrobe has come to take me back to my people."

You see," said Father David to the Sisters, "White Cloud is holding me to my promise."

A few days later, Father David and some helpers started out toward the Red River country. An old Indian squaw went along to take care of White Cloud.

One morning, as they rode over the top of a hill, White Cloud's quick eyes saw some Indians on the green below.

"Let us ride on," she cried. "I am sure they are my people."

Father David told White Cloud to wait at the top of the hill, and he and his helpers rode to meet the Indians.

White Cloud was right! They were the Yohocan Indians, but they had their faces painted black.

This showed that they were sad because someone in their camp had died.

After the priest greeted the Indians, he asked who had died.

"Don't you remember what happened a year ago?" they said. "Some of your friends, the Fox Indians, killed many of our people. They even took our little sister White Cloud from us."

'Have you looked for her?" asked Father David.

"Yes, we have looked," they answered. "We have even sent some of our strongest braves as far as the Fox village to look for her. No one has even seen the child. The Fox have killed her. We shall never see her again."

"Do not say that," said the priest. "I have brought White Cloud back to you."

Then Father David turned to the hill and called, "White Cloud, come down!"

When the little girl came down, she looked for a moment at all the painted faces before her. Then she ran right into the arms of her own father.

The Yohocan Indians could hardly believe what had happened. They all came near the priest. They thought that if they got near him, they would get some of his goodness.

As they rode down to their village, they cried out, "The Blackrobe, our friend, has brought White Cloud back!"

The Pot of Gold

James and his brother Carl were the first white boys to come to live in Yohocan. They quickly made friends with one of the older Indians, who used to tell them stories. One time he told them a story about the pot of gold.

"Anyone who can find the place where the rainbow reaches the earth will find the pot of gold," said the old Indian storyteller.

Grownups knew this was only a fairy story, but James and Carl believed it.

No one wanted to find the pot of gold any more than James and Carl. So, one morning after breakfast, the two boys saw a rainbow and started out to hunt for the pot of gold.

"We will just follow the Indian path through the woods," Carl told his brother. "Then we will not get lost."

On and on down the path the boys walked. They had no clock with them. They tried to guess the time by watching the sun.

In some places, they could hardly find the path. They had to climb over fallen trees and fight their way through bushes. Before long, Carl and James had scratches and cuts all over their legs, hands, and faces, but they did not stop.

"We can't let a few scratches stop us," said Carl.

"We have gone this far, and we must not give up," said James, "not until we reach the end of the rainbow and find the pot of gold."

The boys could no longer see the Indian path because there were so many weeds and bushes over it. But they walked on through the woods.

After a little while, the boys saw water. "A spring!" shouted Carl. "Now for a nice cold drink of water!"

The boys sat down near the spring. How good the cold water felt on their scratched hands, legs, and faces!

Suddenly they heard a strange sound. "What is that?" Carl whispered.

"Only a baby animal or a bird of some kind," answered James. "You are not frightened, are you?"

"Well, not really, I guess," answered Carl. "You don't think there are any unfriendly Indians here, do you?"

"No, all the Indians around here know us," answered James. "I am sure that sound is coming from an animal of some kind. It seems to be over there near those leaves."

"It can't be very large, or we would see it," laughed Carl.

As the two boys watched, they saw one of the bushes move. An Indian boy was coming toward them. He did not say one word. He only gave a sign, showing the white boys that they should keep quiet and not move.

By this time, both Carl and James felt very frightened. "Why does he want us to keep still?" they wondered.

The Indian boy pointed to something under the leaves. It was a snake!

No one said a word. No one moved. After a few minutes, the strange sound stopped.

The Indian boy watched the snake. Then he very carefully stepped around the snake. He gave a sign for the white boys to follow him.

When, at last, they reached a safe place, the Indian began to speak to them. "That kind of snake kills," he told the boys. "It is not safe for you to walk through the woods. I will show you the way back to the village."

As they walked along, the Indian boy taught the two boys many things about finding their way in the big forest.

"Tomorrow, I will teach you how to hunt and fish," promised the boys' new friend.

By the time the boys reached home, it was almost dark. Everyone in the village was out looking for them. There was no scolding, but there were many happy cries when the people saw Carl and James following the Indian boy.

"We could not find the pot of gold," Carl told his parents, "but we found a new friend in the Indian boy."

"And that," said his father, "is far better than all the gold in the world."

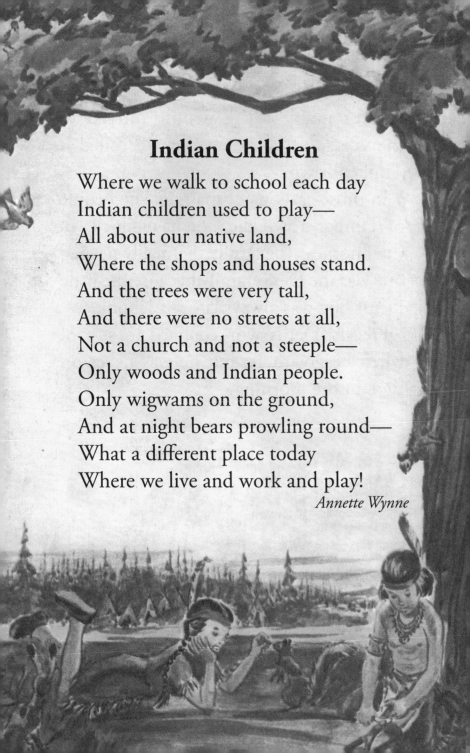

Indian Children

Where we walk to school each day
Indian children used to play—
All about our native land,
Where the shops and houses stand.
And the trees were very tall,
And there were no streets at all,
Not a church and not a steeple—
Only woods and Indian people.
Only wigwams on the ground,
And at night bears prowling round—
What a different place today
Where we live and work and play!

Annette Wynne

The House without a Clock

After many white people moved to the village of Yohocan, they all called it Timber Town.

In those early days, many of the people of Timber Town did not have clocks in their homes. The family that really needed one was the Denis family because the little Denis boy was always late for school.

Freddy Denis worked hard in school when he got there, but he was never on time in the morning.

Freddy could not help this because he really never knew what time it was. He lived with his grandparents, and they did not think they needed a clock.

"Why should we have a clock in this house?" asked Freddy's grandfather.

When it is time to get up, the roosters crow. At milking time, the cows moo. Even the hens and the geese let us know when it is time for them to lay eggs. When the sun goes down, we know it is time to go to bed."

The only trouble was that Freddy did not know when it was time to go to school.

One day a peddler came to the town. The peddler's wagon visited Timber Town about three times a year. It was just like a big store. The peddler brought dishes, pots and pans, thread, pins, vases, coffee, shoes, dolls, seeds, calendars, and even men's suits.

In his wagon, the peddler also had clocks that had been made in a far-away country.

When Grandfather saw the clocks, he said, "I would never trade a rooster for one of those silly new things."

In those days, people did not use money to buy things. They traded things they had for things they did not have.

Timber Town people traded mules, chickens, cows, geese, corn, and things that other people might want or need.

Grandfather did not trade anything, and Freddy still did not have a clock in his house.

Freddy's teacher, Mr. Wells, had almost given up trying to get him to school on time. There was no use scolding or punishing the boy. After all, Freddy could not help being late if there was no clock in his house.

One winter afternoon, Mr. Wells went home with Freddy and asked Freddy's grandparents to get a clock.

"Just where on earth do you think we would ever get a clock at this time of year?" Grandmother asked the teacher.

"I'm not sure I want a clock," said Grandfather. "A rooster was good enough for me when I was a boy."

After a few months, spring came back to Timber Town. One bright Saturday morning, the peddler's horn was heard. All the women had been waiting for this very exciting day. They had all kinds of things to trade for other things they wanted from the peddler.

"What do you have in your wagon?" asked one woman after another.

"Fifty fine clocks!" cried the peddler. "Some of the finest clocks in the world!"

"Nothing but clocks?" said the women. "Why, we have had clocks in this village for over three years. Almost everyone has a clock." Then the women walked slowly back to their houses.

Now, no one knew that Freddy Denis and his two pet pigs were hiding under the peddler's wagon. After all the older people had left, Freddy came out from his hiding place.

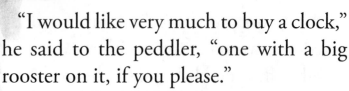

"I would like very much to buy a clock," he said to the peddler, "one with a big rooster on it, if you please."

The peddler laughed. "Now, how do you think a little boy like you could ever buy one of these fine clocks?" he asked.

"With these two fine pigs," answered Freddy, as he showed his pet pigs.

"Well, they are the finest two pigs I have ever seen," cried the peddler. "I'll give you my very finest clock with a rooster painted on it."

Freddy took the clock and ran home as fast as he could. His family was so very surprised to hear what he had done. Grandfather set the clock. Soon it began to strike at every hour.

"Maybe a clock is a good thing to have after all," laughed Grandmother.

It was very good for Freddy because he was never again late for school.

Hildegard Woodward

Getting Together Again

The boys and girls of Timber Town had fun playing together. They also found time to work and help others, just as the grownups did.

Here are some more stories about things that happened in their town.

Prince Comes to Town

Rainy days had come to Timber Town. It had rained so much that parts of the town were flooded. Many places had been closed. Even the schools were closed.

Matt Lake and Peter Martin had not seen their space brother, Jan Cook, for about a week. Early one morning, they tried to reach him by telephone, but no one answered. This made Matt and Peter wonder about their friend.

"I wonder if anything has happened to Jan," said Peter. "Do you think that maybe his house has been flooded?"

"If that happened, where would Jan go?" asked Matt.

"I guess he would have to climb to the top of his roof," Peter replied.

"Poor Jan," said Matt. "Maybe he's sitting up there right now. Maybe he is cold and hungry."

"We must find our space brother," said Peter. "It has stopped raining. Why don't we walk over to our space station and see if he is there?"

The two boys put on their raincoats, hats, and boots and walked toward the field.

As they walked along, they met the mailman. "What are you boys doing out in weather like this?" asked the mailman. "This weather is much better for ducks than for people."

Matt replied, "We are out looking for our friend. We don't know what has happened to him."

"What does he look like?" asked the mailman.

"He's about as tall as we are," replied Peter, "and he has blue eyes and black hair."

"Oh, I saw a boy like that a little while ago," said the mailman. "Does he wear a yellow raincoat and ride a horse?"

The boys shook their heads. "He might be riding a bicycle," answered Matt, "but I'm sure he would never be riding a horse."

"Well, I hope you find your friend," said the mailman as he walked away.

"Say, look at the river!" cried Matt as he climbed up into their space station. "It really is flooded."

"Look at all the things floating in the river," said Peter, pointing to a big log bobbing along in the water.

"Poor Jan," said Matt. "I hope the water isn't over the top of his house."

"He may even be floating down the river on a log," said Peter.

"Who's floating down the river on a log?" a voice asked.

The boys looked down and could hardly believe their own eyes. There was Jan! He wasn't sitting on top of his flooded house. He wasn't floating down the river on a log.

Jan was right there below them—sitting on a big horse!

"Jan, you are safe!" both boys shouted at once.

"Of course," Jan replied. "What made you think I was not?"

When the boys told Jan what they had been thinking, he laughed and laughed.

"Everyone in my family is fine," he said, "and our house is safe. While you have been wondering about me, I've been looking for you. I wanted to give you a ride on Prince."

"Where in the world did you get a horse?" asked Matt.

"He belongs to my uncle," said Jan.

"Where is your uncle?" asked Peter.

"My uncle is helping the men down by the river bank," said Jan. "They are putting sandbags along the river to keep the water back so it will not flood the buildings. My uncle rode Prince into town today.

"Prince is a farm horse and is used to hard work. Climb on. He is big and strong enough to carry all three of us," Jan boasted.

"That's great!" said Peter. He climbed down and sat behind Jan and held on to him. Matt sat behind Peter and held on to him.

"Let's go, Prince!" said Jan proudly.

"This is more fun than playing space ship," Peter said. "Now we are really going places."

The Singing Errand

The three space brothers liked to sing.
They each had songs that they liked best,
but all three liked "The Boat Song."

Sometimes they rode their bicycles along
the streets, singing this song at the tops of
their voices:

> "Speed on, good boat,
> Like a bird on the wing.
> Speed on!" the boatmen cry.

> "Carry the boy
> That's born to be king.
> Carry him on!" they cry.

The faster the boys rode, the louder they sang. Sometimes they would almost forget that they were Timber Town boys riding through the streets on their bicycles.

They thought they were brave boatmen on a far-off sea, rowing their boats in very bad weather.

The boys knew that "The Boat Song" told a story about some brave boatmen who once saved the life of a prince.

The prince was named Charlie. Now, most of the people loved him, but there were others who wanted to kill him.

One time Prince Charlie's enemies were looking for him. Some friendly boatmen put the prince into their boat to take him to a safe country far across the sea.

The rain came down, and the wind blew. But the brave boatmen rowed across the angry waters and saved Prince Charlie.

One day while the boys were singing, Peter said, "I wish we could find a boat. To sing 'The Boat Song' in the right way, we should be rowing a boat."

"If we can't have a boat, maybe we can ride a horse," said Jan. "I think my uncle will let us have Prince."

"It will be hard trying to make believe that Prince is a boat," said Matt, "but it will be more fun than riding bicycles."

The boys went to Jan's uncle, who was glad to let them take Prince.

They rode along the street, singing:
"Speed on, good boat,
Like a bird on the wing."

"Prince seems proud to be called a good boat," said Jan as he rubbed his hand over the horse's head.

"I wish we could save someone's life," Matt said, "someone great like the prince the song tells about."

The boys were riding by a large red building when they heard someone call, "Say, where are you going?"

It was a cook, looking out of one of the windows of the building.

"We are on our way to find someone to save," answered Jan.

"Good! Very good!" laughed the cook. "You have found someone right here."

"Where?" asked all three boys at once.

The cook pointed to himself and said, "I have been waiting for someone to take a basket of food to the sandbag workers. If they don't get it soon, they may come up here and eat me."

"We'll be glad to carry the food down to the workers," laughed Peter.

In a few minutes, the cook came out, carrying a large basket. When he handed it to the boys, he said, "Be careful. There's a pot of hot coffee in there."

The cook thanked the boys, and they rode off, singing at the top of their voices.

"Well, this is one way to be brave and to help others," laughed Matt.

The sandbag workers were hungry and very pleased to get the basket of food.

The men thanked the boys, but Peter said, "Prince, our good horse, did most of the work. He's as good as the boat that saved Prince Charlie."

A Strange Surprise

"Wait for us," cried Peggy Martin and Melissa Lake as they ran to catch up with their brothers and Jan Cook.

Many times the five children played together and had good times together.

"Hurry up!" said Peter to the girls. "We are going over to the park to play."

Timber Town Park was on a hillside near the river.

"Look!" shouted Melissa just after they had reached the park: "There's a cave!"

"How exciting!" cried Peggy.

"Let's go inside!" cried Melissa, but her brother Matt held her back.

"We boys will go in first," Matt told her. "It might be a dangerous place."

"Yes, there might even be wild bears in this cave," said Jan, trying to frighten the girls.

"Bears like caves, you know," Peter told the girls. "At the zoo, they have caves for the bears to live in so that they will feel at home."

Peter knew this because he and his sister Peggy had once gone to the zoo far up the river.

"Well, anyway, I'm sure there are no bears in this cave," laughed Melissa. "I saw the cave first, and I'm going to be the first one to go in."

"I don't think girls should go into dangerous places like this," said Jan.

Melissa did not listen. She went right into the cave. The boys went in behind Melissa. Peggy was last because she felt frightened.

Peter said, "I think Old One Eye, the king of the bears, is hiding in here."

"I can hear him growl," Matt whispered.

The girls began to feel a little more frightened.

"I can see his one eye. Why, he must be as large as an elephant," said Peter. "Oh, how very hungry he looks! How dangerous!"

"You girls had better get out of here," said Jan. "Old One Eye may strike at you any minute."

"I found the cave first, and I won't get out," said Melissa, who sometimes wanted her own way.

Suddenly the children heard a strange sound. It was a real sound, not just a make-believe one.

"What is that?" said Peter as he took hold of Jan's arm.

Matt whispered quickly, "I believe there really is something alive in here."

"Maybe it's a real bear!" said Peggy.

"Listen!" Jan said suddenly.

The children stopped talking. They listened. They heard the sound again. It was something like a deep growl.

Melissa held her head high. "I'm not frightened," she said.

The sound was heard again. Matt took out a small flashlight which he had in his pocket. He turned it on and moved it around in the dark cave.

"Look!" he whispered.

The flashlight showed two eyes, away back in a corner of the cave.

"Eyes!" whispered Matt. "Real eyes!" "Let me out of here!" said Melissa, running as fast as she could.

"Me too!" said Peggy. "It's too spooky in here."

The boys took a few more steps toward the corner. Now they could see a small animal in the back of the cave.

"I believe it's a cat or maybe a kitten," whispered Jan.

Peter reached his hand out toward the small animal. The animal did not growl any more. It made a sound like a baby crying.

"It's not a cat," laughed Jan. "It's a puppy. It's just a lost, frightened puppy."

Matt looked. "You're wrong! There are two puppies," he said.

As Matt held the flashlight, Jan and Peter each took one of the animals. Then the three boys hurried out of the cave.

"Oh, what pretty little puppies!" cried Melissa when the boys came out of the cave.

Peggy looked at the little animals. "Those are not puppies," she said in a strange voice.

"I believe they are real bear cubs. I have seen some at the zoo," she said.

"You are just trying to frighten us," said Melissa. "Bears are big and wild and hungry-looking. These are just little puppies."

"Let's find out," said Jan. "We can ask someone who knows."

The five children walked along a path. Before long, they met a policeman. The policeman looked at them and rubbed his eyes. Then he looked again.

"Where did you get those bear cubs?" he asked.

All five children spoke at once. The policeman listened to their story.

Then he said, "I believe I know what has happened. The cubs were washed out of the zoo the other day when it rained so hard. Some of the other wild animals were lost in the rain and high water, too."

The policeman took one of the little new-born cubs. "These poor little bears are hungry," he said, "but you have saved their lives."

The policeman whistled to a police car. He took the children and the cubs to the police station. There they fed the hungry little animals.

After the bears had had some milk, they lay down and went to sleep.

"We will take the bears back to the zoo tomorrow," said the policeman.

That evening, the newspaper showed a picture of the five children with the bear cubs. There was a story about how the children had found the new-born cubs.

Everyone at River Street School was proud of Jan Cook, and everyone at St. Francis School was proud of Peter and Peggy Martin and of Matt and Melissa Lake. The five hunters were proudest of all.

A Fine Mix-Up

Jan Cook was riding his wagon down to the street corner when Mrs. Brooks, one of the neighbors, called him.

"Jan," said Mrs. Brooks in an excited voice, "my aunt who lives in Twin City is sick and wants me to come and stay with her for a while. I'll have to leave on the next bus. Do you think you could take care of a few errands for me?"

"Yes," answered. Jan. "I was only going to the store to buy a new headlight for my bicycle, but that can wait."

Mrs. Brooks took Jan into her kitchen. On the table were three boxes that all looked the same.

"I had planned to get these to the right people today," she told Jan. This first box is for your mother. The second one is for Mrs. Burns. It is maple sugar candy. If Mrs. Burns is not home, tell whoever opens the door to put the box on ice."

Mrs. Brooks gave Jan another box. "I don't know what is in here," she said.

"The man who gave it to me just asked me to see that Mrs. Rose got it today."

Then Mrs. Brooks wrote the names of the three people on three small pieces of paper and put each paper on the right box. She did this so Jan could remember where to leave the boxes.

"Good-by, Mrs. Brooks," said Jan. "I hope your aunt will be better soon. Don't worry about these packages. I'll take care of them right away."

Just as Jan started down the street, the pieces of paper blew off the boxes. He picked them up and put them back again.

Mrs. Burns and Mrs. Rose did not live very far away. So Jan took their packages to them first. Then he went home and gave his mother hers.

Jan's mother did not open the box. "Those are my cards that Mrs. Brooks used, for her card party last week," she said. "We won't need them for a while. So just put the box in the closet."

That evening, Mrs. Rose came to see Jan's mother. "I have something funny to tell you," she said. "You know little Timmy who lives next door to us, don't you? Well, I planned to surprise him with a pet turtle for his birthday. So I asked the man at the store to send me one through Mrs. Brooks. Someone brought a package to our house this morning while I was away.

"My son thought it was a pet turtle and should be put in a warm place."

Mrs. Rose laughed again. "When I came home, I saw something coming out of the box. It wasn't a pet turtle. It was maple syrup!" she said.

"Maple syrup!" said Jan's mother at once. "How did that happen?"

"Well, I guess the man at the store just got things mixed up," said Mrs. Rose, "and put maple sugar candy in the box and not a turtle. When the candy got warm, it turned into syrup."

All this time Jan had been listening. Mrs. Rose had just left the house when the telephone in the kitchen started ringing. It was Mrs. Burns. She had something to tell Jan's mother.

In a few minutes, Jan's mother called him from the kitchen. "That box you put in the closet could not have playing cards in it," she said. "Mrs. Burns just called to say that she found playing cards in the ice box and no maple sugar candy."

Jan ran to the closet to get the box. What a surprise he had when he opened it and saw a turtle!

"I must have mixed up the pieces of paper with the names on them when they blew off the boxes," he told his mother.

"Well, not too much harm has been done," said Mrs. Cook. "The turtle is alive. The playing cards were not harmed by being on ice. All we need is some maple sugar candy for Mrs. Burns."

Mrs. Cook said that a new box of maple sugar candy would cost a dollar. Jan had two dollars and a dime in his bank.

So by the time Mrs. Brooks came back from Twin City, everything was fixed up.

Jeannette Covert Nolan

The New Parish

St. Francis Church was too small for all the people who belonged to the parish.

One day the Timber Town people learned that a new parish was to be made. All those living west of the river would belong to the new parish. It would be called the Blessed Sacrament Parish.

"Will we belong to the new parish, Daddy?" Melissa Lake asked her father.

"Yes, we will," replied Mr. Lake. "Your friends Peter and Peggy Martin will, too, because we all live west of the river."

"I'm glad that they will belong to the Blessed Sacrament Parish," said Matt. "Where is our new church?"

"We won't have a church for a while," answered Mr. Lake. "When our new pastor comes, he will have to find a place in which to offer Mass until we can build a church."

Then Mrs. Lake began to speak. "The new pastor is coming to town Tuesday morning," she said. "All the grownups will meet him at a get-together party on Wednesday evening."

On Tuesday morning, Matt and Peter went to serve at the eight o'clock Mass. Just as they were going into the church, Father Carl called them.

"Boys, the new pastor of the Blessed Sacrament Parish will offer the eight o'clock Mass this morning," he said. "He may be a little late. Just sit down and wait until he comes."

The boys did as they had been told. Then, after a few minutes, the door opened. Matt and Peter had the surprise of their lives.

They jumped up and cried, "Oh, it's Father Michaels! It's Father Michaels!"

"Are you the pastor of the new Blessed. Sacrament Parish?" asked Peter.

"Yes, I am," laughed the priest as he started shaking hands with the boys. "We never thought this would happen when we met at the airport some months ago, did we?"

On the following Sunday, the people of the Blessed Sacrament Parish went to Mass in a strange place. It was not a beautiful church like St. Francis Church. It really was not a church at all. It was a theater on Fourth Street.

It seemed strange, very strange, to see an altar in the old theater. After the Mass began, most people forgot about being in the theater. The Mass is the same anywhere it is offered. That made the people feel at home.

Peter and Matt were serving the Mass.

"How good and kind Our Lord is," Peter thought. "He does not seem to care where He is, just as long as He can offer Himself to His Father as a sacrifice for our sins."

"We don't even have a church, and yet we can have the Mass," thought Matt as he knelt before the altar. "Jesus is willing to offer Himself as a sacrifice to His Father, even in a place like this.

"How nice it will be when we have a pretty new church of our own."

After Mass, Father Michaels spoke to the people. "We will have Mass here in the theater every Sunday until we can build our new church," he told them.

"We can begin to build soon, if you are willing to help with the work."

The pastor did not have to wait long for willing workers. "We will do all that we can to help," the people said.

Men offered to work every evening and all day on Saturdays. They would put up the building themselves.

Some of the men offered to do the wood work, and others offered to do the stone work. Some said they would take care of the painting.

Father Michaels was pleased with the goodness of his people. Already they had worked hard for St. Francis Church. Now they were willing to put up another building in which they could pray and offer sacrifice to God.

A Special Day in March

All the people of Blessed Sacrament Parish worked very hard building their new church.

"Our church is almost finished," Father Michaels told the people one Sunday. "But a new church cannot be used until it has been blessed.

"I just received a letter from our bishop saying that he will come to bless our church on the first Sunday in March."

On Monday, the Timber Town newspaper showed pictures of the new church and told about the bishop coming to bless it.

In the next few weeks, everyone seemed to be happy and very busy. Men were helping to clean the church. Women were busy sewing new altar cloths. The school children were learning how to greet the bishop. The boys in the Timber Town Band were learning some new music.

When Peter got up on the first Sunday in March, he heard some strange sounds outside. Someone was playing a horn.

Peter ran to the window and looked out. There were his friends, Jan, Matt, and some other boys.

"You had better hurry," Matt cried to Peter. "Do you know it is half-past seven, and we are to be down at the hall by eight o'clock?"

Peter hurried because he did not want to be late on a special day like this. He and Matt were to serve the bishop's Mass. Both boys felt proud and excited.

As soon as Peter was ready, the boys hurried down to the hall near the new church. That is where all the children were to meet. From there, they started walking to the priest's house to meet the bishop.

When the bishop saw all the people, he could hardly believe his eyes. "I thought it was only a small town," he whispered to Father Michaels. "Where did all these people come from?"

Father Michaels told the bishop that many friends who did not belong to the parish had come to join in the blessing.

Jan was in the Merry Music Makers' Club so he walked to the priest's house with the band. Peter and Matt were dressed in their servers' clothes.

Melissa and Peggy were flower girls. They carried a large basket of lovely pink roses.

There was not enough room in the new church for all the people. Some of them had to stand outside while the bishop blessed the altars and offered the sacrifice of the Mass. The bishop spoke to them through a loudspeaker so that all could hear.

"You, the people of Timber Town, have lived and worked together just as real children of God," he told them. "Surely our heavenly Father must be pleased to see how you help one another.

"May God bless your homes and families, your fine town, and this new parish!"

Then the music started, and all the people sang "Holy God."

They were happy and thankful that there was another beautiful house of God in Timber Town. It was the work of their own hands. So they felt that it was theirs in a very special way.

God's Homes

I know that God is everywhere
And all about us—like the air!

God lives in heaven, away up high
Above the earth and air and sky.

To share our little joys and tears,
He lived on earth for thirty years.

In every Mass He comes again;
His joy is still to dwell with men.

And when I go to church, He's there—
He says it is His "House of Prayer."

God lives in every soul in grace,
And makes of it a holy place;

Within my heart, though none can see,
Lives God—He is at home with me!

E. S.

The Tell-a-Tale Club

Many boys and girls of Timber Town belonged to a book club which was called the Tell-a-Tale Club. At meetings, children told about library books they had read. Sometimes prizes were given to those who had read the most and the best books.

Here are some of the stories that were read by the children in the club.

Apron Troubles

There was once a Little Old Woman who needed a new apron, but she had no money to buy one.

"If only I had a nice piece of cloth, I could make an apron," she thought. "Then a new apron would not cost anything. I will look through my bag of scrap goods and see what I can find."

So she got out her bag of scrap goods and put on her glasses. Then she sat down to look for a piece of cloth to make herself an apron.

First she pulled out a small piece of blue cloth. "This would make a fine pocket," she said, "but what good would an apron pocket be without an apron?"

The Little Old Woman pulled a long piece of red cloth out of the scrap bag.

"This would make fine apron strings," she said, "but what good would apron strings be without an apron?"

There was a large piece of black cloth in the bag. When the Little Old Woman saw it, she said, 'This would make a fine apron, but it is too long. Half of it would be on the ground. And what good is an apron if half of it is on the ground?"

She pulled out one piece of cloth after another. Some were too short, and some were too long. Some pieces were too wide, and some were not wide enough.

At last, there was only one piece of cloth left in the scrap bag. It was a pretty piece of green cloth with little yellow flowers on it.

"This is a very fine piece of cloth," said the Little Old Woman. "It isn't too wide, and it isn't too long. But it is just a little too short."

She tried to think of a way to make the piece of cloth longer. After she thought and thought, she said, "I need another piece of cloth just like this to make a ruffle. Then I could put the ruffle on the bottom of the apron to make it longer. Now, where can I get another piece of cloth just like this?"

Then she said, "This will take some thinking. I shall have to use my head."

The Little Old Woman got a cloth and put water on it to make it wet. She put the wet cloth around her head.

Then she sat down with her finger on her nose and closed her eyes. This is what the Little Old Woman always did when she used her head to think.

She used her head, and she used her head. Soon she knew where to get a piece of green cloth with yellow flowers on it.

"I will cut a piece off the top of the apron," she said. "Then I will make a ruffle with it and sew it to the bottom of the apron to make it longer. What a wise Little Old Woman I am!"

So she cut off a piece from the top of the apron and made a ruffle. She sewed the ruffle to the bottom of the apron to make it longer.

When the apron was finished, the Little Old Woman put it on and went to the looking glass to see how it looked.

It was easy to see that the apron was shorter than ever.

"Dear me," she said. "Who would have thought that a ruffle could make an apron shorter? I've always said you can learn something new every day of your life if you only use your head."

Hope Newell

The Wonderful Inventor

Mr. Buttercup was a wonderful inventor, and he was just as kind and as wise as he could be. He used all his time inventing things to make life easier for people. Of course, he made people much happier, too.

He invented machines that washed and ironed clothes and even sewed patches on them. One of his machines took people's shoes off for them. It could put the shoes back on again, too.

He made a new self-making bed and a telephone that answered itself.

Now, all these wonderful things made Mr. Buttercup a very rich man, but he was also a very tired man. What he needed most was a good rest.

One day, Mr. Buttercup found a little house on a quiet little farm on a quiet little road in a quiet little town. He went there to take a good long rest.

He had rested only ten minutes on the front steps of his new little house when he saw some pigs running through a field. One little pig could not run very fast because his legs were so short.

At once, Mr. Buttercup began to think of something to make the pig run faster.

He made four stilts for the pig's legs. He caught the pig and put one stilt on each leg.

Away ran the pig on his stilts—through the yard and through the field, just as fast as the other pigs.

"Those stilts make me think of many other things I could invent for other animals," said Mr. Buttercup. "I have always worked to make life easier for people. Now I want to help animals."

So first, Mr. Buttercup invented a prettier and larger hat for the horses to wear when the sun was hot.

He invented a fly swatter that helped the horses to keep the flies and other bugs off. As the fly swatter worked, it made a little breeze which helped to keep the horses cool.

One day, he invented little sails for the ducks to help them swim in the pond.

He made a machine that fed grass to the cows. Then they no longer had to walk around all day looking for food.

In the end, all these things did more harm than good. The horses were so free and had so little to do that they jumped over the fence and ate all the neighbor's corn. The corn made them very, very sick.

The sails turned the ducks around so fast that they could not walk right when they came out of the water.

The cows liked their old way of getting grass. They soon disliked the machine that fed them. They became angry and ran out of the barn into the neighbor's newly planted field and stepped all over his carrot and pumpkin plants. They ran through Mrs. Fay's yard and pulled down the clean clothes she had just washed.

"My, oh, my!" said Mr. Buttercup.

"This will never do!"

He called all the animals together. He put all the things that he had made for them into a large box. Then he made a machine to get rid of the things he had invented.

He got rid of the horses' fly swatters and hats. He got rid of the sails he had made for the ducks. He got rid of the machine that fed the cows.

Then, at last, Mr. Buttercup had a good long rest.

Helen and Alf Evers

The Wrong Side of the Bed

One cool morning, Aunt Milly sat up in bed and looked around. She rubbed her eyes and looked around again.

Just then her clock began to strike: one, two, three, four, five, six.

"Dear me!" cried Aunt Milly, jumping out of bed. "It's six o'clock! I must get dressed at once!"

Aunt Milly always got up at five, fed the chickens, and had her own breakfast by six. It was not often that she stayed in bed so long.

So she started dressing in a hurry. As soon as she had finished, she went downstairs to fix breakfast. But as Aunt Milly walked, her feet felt very strange. They seemed to be going the wrong way.

Aunt Milly looked down at her shoes. She had them on the wrong feet.

"Well, now, what do you think of that?" she said. "I'm surely getting off to a bad start today."

Aunt Milly had just changed her shoes when she heard strange sounds coming from the next room. She hurried to see what was happening.

There was her pet parrot, all mixed up in a ball of string.

"Well, forevermore!" cried Aunt Milly. "How on earth did you get that string?"

The parrot had never learned to talk, and so he could not say anything.

Aunt Milly went on, "Just wait, and I'll help you."

She began to cut the string. She cut so fast that she even cut off some of the parrot's pretty green tail.

"Everything bad seems to be happening today," she told the parrot.

Suddenly there was a cloud of dust outside. Mr. Rooster, the hens, and chicks were having breakfast in Aunt Milly's garden.

"Get out of there!" Aunt Milly called as she ran out, waving her arms at the chickens. They were frightened and flew away as fast as they could.

Then Aunt Milly remembered that she had not yet had her breakfast. She hurried into the house and filled the coffee pot with water. She put some rolls in to bake and put an egg into a pan.

"Toot, toot, toot!" came a sound from outside.

"What next?" cried Aunt Milly. She went to the door, and there stood the mail truck.

"A letter for you!" said the mailman. Then he asked, "Whatever is wrong with you today, Aunt Milly? You don't look like yourself."

"Everything is wrong," replied Aunt Milly. And she told the mailman all her troubles.

"Maybe you got up on the wrong side of the bed this morning," he laughed. "That can make everything go wrong."

After the mailman left, Aunt Milly opened her letter and started to read it. Suddenly, she remembered the egg, coffee, and rolls. So she ran to see about her breakfast.

"Well, I give up!" she cried as she looked into the pan. The egg was burned black. The rolls were as flat as pancakes. She had forgotten to put yeast in them.

"I'm sure there is something wrong with the coffee, too," thought Aunt Milly. She was right.

When she looked into the pot, she saw only water in it. She had forgotten to put in the coffee.

"I wonder if the mailman was right," said Aunt Milly. "Maybe I did get up on the wrong side of the bed. I had better do something about it."

She went up to her bedroom, pulled off her apron and dress, and put on her night clothes. Then she got into bed and closed her eyes.

When the clock began to strike ten, she climbed out of bed. This time she was very careful to get out on the other side of the bed.

She put her shoes on the right feet. She looked out of the window, and the chickens were where they belonged.

Then she went downstairs and made breakfast all over again. This time the egg was just right. The rolls were not flat. The coffee was sweet and just as strong as Aunt Milly wanted it to be.

"Everything seems to be all right now," she said.

Then she remembered the letter which the mailman had given her that morning. She hurried to get the letter.

It was from her brother who lived in the city. He wanted her to stay with him and his family for a few days. He even sent a plane ticket for her to use.

"Wonderful!" said Aunt Milly. "I'll ask some of my neighbors to take care of my chickens and the parrot. It will be fun to be in the city for a few days."

Ollie James Robertson

The Bread Cloud

Once there were three bakers named Buffy, Tuffy, and Stuffy who baked the best bread anyone had ever eaten.

Every day, Buffy would say good-by to his wife, climb on his bicycle, and ride to work.

And every day, Tuffy would say good-by to *his* wife, climb on *his* bicycle, and ride to work.

And every day, Stuffy would say good-by to *his* wife, climb on *his* bicycle, and ride to work.

At work, Buffy would mix the flour with water to make the bread for the bakery. Tuffy would put in the sugar to make the bread sweet. Stuffy would put in yeast to make the bread fluffy, puffy, and light.

In that way, each baker had one thing to do, and he always did it just right. While the bakers worked, they sang:

"Bread that's light,
Bread that's sweet,
Bread that's puffy,
And good to eat.
We mix the flour
With sugar and yeast,
So buy our bread
And have a feast."

Every day, many people would come to their bakery to buy the bread. There would be big people and small people, short people and tall people—all standing in their bakery buying bread.

One morning, when the sun came out, Buffy got up, said good-by to his wife, got on his bicycle, and rode to work.

Tuffy said good-by to *his* wife, got on *his* bicycle, and rode to work.

And Stuffy said good-by to *his* wife, got on *his* bicycle, and started to ride to work.

But when Stuffy was halfway to work, his bicycle broke down, and he had to carry it all the rest of the way.

Poor Stuffy! He would never get to the bakery on time today. And who would put the yeast in the bread?

"I hope that Buffy or Tuffy will put the yeast in the bread," he said, "because without yeast, the bread will be flat and as hard as a cracker. It will not get fluffy, puffy, and light."

While Stuffy was still carrying his bicycle to work, Buffy was already at the bakery mixing the flour and water.

"My goodness, it is late," he said. "Maybe Stuffy will not come to work today. Then who will put the yeast in the bread? I know. I'll put the yeast in the bread."

Buffy did not know that you need only a little yeast to make the bread fluffy, puffy, and light. So Buffy put in too much.

When Tuffy was putting in the sugar to make the bread sweet, he said, "My goodness, it is late. Maybe Stuffy will not come to work today. Then who will put the yeast in the bread? I know. I'll put the yeast in the bread."

Tufty did not know how much yeast to put in, and he put in much too much.

Stuffy reached the bakery just before the bread was put into the oven.

"Just in time!" said Stuffy to himself, and he added just enough yeast to make the bread just fluffy, puffy, and light enough.

Of course, he did not know that Buffy and Tuffy had already put in much too much yeast.

While the bread was in the oven being baked, it got bigger and bigger and bigger. It got so big that it filled all of the oven. It pushed the oven door open and went all over the floor.

It got so big that it filled all of the bakery and went out of the door into the street. It got so big that it went down the street and all over the grass in the park.

And while it got bigger, it also got fluffier and puffier and lighter.

All the big people and the small people and the short people and the tall people watched it get fluffier and puffier and lighter and lighter and lighter until it was as light as a balloon.

All the people watched as a breeze made it float up, up, up, right into the sky. And there it was—a great, big bread cloud!

So Buffy, Tuffy, and Stuffy had no bread to sell in their bakery that day.

After that, every morning Buffy would say good-by to his wife, look up in the sky at the bread cloud, get on his bicycle, and ride to work.

And Tuffy and Stuffy did the same thing. But Stuffy was very careful to get to work on time.

He knew that he must add the yeast to the bread because he didn't want the bread to get too fluffy, too puffy, and too light to stay in the bakery.

Lois Salk Galpern

The Wonderful Brass Pot

There once was an old man and an old woman who had no food and no money. They had only one goat. So they planned to sell the goat and get some money.

As the old man walked to the village with the goat, he met a young man who wanted to buy it from him.

"How much do you want for the goat?" the young man asked.

"I want ten dollars or maybe more," replied the old man. "She's a very fine goat as you can see."

"I don't have any money, but I have something worth more than money," said the young man. He opened a bag and took out a little brass pot with four short legs.

"I'm sorry," said the old man, "but I cannot give you this fine goat for that little brass pot."

Then a strange thing happened. The little pot began to sing:

> "I'm very clever,
> As you will see.
> If you take me home,
> Happy you'll be."

The old man was very much surprised.

"Of course, I'll take a wonderful little pot like that," he told the young man.

So the young man took the goat, and the old man took the little brass pot.

On his way, home the old man began to worry. He was afraid his wife would not like the pot.

When the old man got home, his wife asked at once, "Did you get much money for our goat?"

The little old man was afraid to tell his wife what he had done. He knew they needed the money very badly.

"I have something that's worth much more than money," he told her. Then he showed her the little brass pot.

"What nonsense!" said the old woman when she saw the little brass pot. "That is worth nothing at all to us."

Just then the little pot began to sing:

> "Rub me and rub me
> Until I am bright.
> Put me over the fire,
> And I'll do what is right."

"It does seem to be a wonderful magic pot," the old woman said when she heard the pot singing.

The old woman washed the pot and rubbed it with her fingers and hands until it was bright. Then she put it on the fire. And what do you think happened?

The little pot jumped down to the floor. It jumped out of the door, and down the road it went, bump, bump, bump on its short legs. It went right into a rich man's house.

Now, this greedy rich man had taken everything away from the poor old man and woman. That was why they had no food and no money.

The rich man's wife was busy making apple dumplings. When she saw the little brass pot, she said, "That is just what I need for my dumplings."

So she put sugar, flour, butter, and apples together and made some dumplings. When the dumplings were ready, she put them into the little pot.

As soon as the pot was full, it jumped off the table. Through the door it went and down the road, bump, bump, bump on its little short legs, all the way to the old man's house.

"What a clever little pot you are!" cried the old woman when she saw the little brass pot filled with dumplings.

The old woman put the dumplings on the fire to cook. That evening the old man and his wife had a wonderful feast.

The next day, the old woman washed the pot again. She rubbed it and put it on the fire.

At that very minute the little pot began to sing:

> "I hop, I hop,
> And I won't stop
> Until you have wheat
> Of your own to eat."

Then the pot jumped to the floor and out of the door. Bump, bump, bump it went right to the rich man's barn.

In no time at all, the little pot was back filled to the top with wheat. Every day after that, the pot did something wonderful for the poor man and his wife.

One day when the two old people were sitting in front of the fire, the little pot began to jump around.

Then the little pot began to sing:
"That greedy rich man
    Took away all your gold.
    But today I'll bring back
    All I can hold."
Out the door and down the road went
the little brass pot, bump, bump, bump.

In a minute, it was right on top of the
rich man's table.

The greedy rich man was putting his
money into bags. When he saw the brass
pot, he said, "What luck! This is just what
I need for all my money."

He began to put the gold into the pot.

Now, the pot was small, but it was magic. So it could hold all the money the man put into it.

As soon as the pot was filled, it gave one big jump and went out the window.

When the brass pot got to the poor man's house, the old man called to his wife, "Oh, come and see what we have! Now we shall never be poor again."

At last the old people had back all their gold that the greedy man had taken.

After that, the little pot was quiet for a long time. Then one day, when the old woman was washing it, the pot surprised her with a new song.

"I'll hop once more
To the rich man's door."

Down the road went the little pot. When the rich man saw it, he cried, "Oh, there you are. You took my dumplings, my wheat, and my gold. This time you will not get away."

Just as he reached to take hold of the pot, the little pot caught the greedy man. It began to pull him out of the house and down the road.

The pot ran so fast that no one could catch up with it. And all the way, it pulled the rich man after it.

Where it went, no one knows. From that day to this, no one ever again saw the clever little brass pot or the greedy rich man.

Scandinavian Folk Tale

Willy's Fine Fiddle
Off to Town

Once upon a time, there was a poor boy named Willy, who worked for a very rich man. Now all the rich man promised to give Willy for his work was brown bread to eat, a bed to sleep on, and one penny a year. In those days a penny, was worth more than it is now.

After Willy had worked for the man for three years, he wanted to leave. So he asked for his pennies.

The rich man became angry, and he said, "Take them, and be off with you!"

With the three pennies in his pocket, Willy started walking toward town. He wanted to buy some new clothes because his clothes were very, very ragged.

Every once in a while, Willy stopped, sat by the road, and counted his pennies. He wanted to be sure he had not lost any of them.

Once, while he was counting his pennies, a poor man came along the road. The man was so big that Willy cried out when he saw him.

"Do not be afraid," said the poor man. "Harm you I will not. I came only to ask you for a penny."

"I have only three pennies," said Willy, "and I need them to buy some clothes."

"Not even one penny have I," said the poor man, "and my clothes are much more ragged than yours."

"That is so," said Willy. And he gave the man one of the three pennies that he had.

Willy went on down the road toward town. After a while, he grew tired. and sat down to rest by a fir tree. Again Willy started to count his pennies. Once again a poor man came along the road. This poor man was also very big. He asked Willy for a penny.

"I have only two pennies," said Willy. "I need them to buy some clothes, for my clothes are very ragged."

"Not even one penny have I," said the poor man, "and for sure, my clothes are much more ragged than yours."

"That is so," said Willy. And he gave the man one of the two pennies that he had left.

Willy went on down the road. After a while he grew so tired that he sat down again to rest. Just then along came another poor man. So very, very big was he that Willy was very frightened when he saw him.

"Do not be afraid," said the poor man. "I will not harm you. I came only to ask you for a penny."

"But I have already given away two pennies," said Willy. "Now I have only one penny left to buy some clothes. As you see, my clothes are very ragged."

"Not even one penny have I," said the man, "and my clothes, you can see, are much more ragged than yours."

"That is true," said Willy. And he gave his last penny to the man.

Then the man said something that made Willy very happy. "You are a good boy, Willy," he said. "You gave away all you had. Now for each of your three pennies, you may have a wish."

All his life, Willy had wanted a fiddle. So he said, "My first wish is that I may have the very finest fiddle on earth."

"That is a poor wish," said the man, "but you may have it. For your second wish, you must think of something better."

"My second wish is that I may play my fiddle so well that everyone who hears it will dance," said Willy.

"That is a poor wish, too," said the man, "but you may have it. You must think of something better and more important for your last wish."

"My last wish is that no one can say 'No' to anything I ask," said Willy.

"Well, that wish is not such a poor one," said the man, and away he went.

Willy's Good Luck

When Willy got to town, he found that no one could say "No" to anything he asked. The man at the clothing store could not say "No," and he gave Willy some fine new clothes. The man at the shoe shop could not say "No," and he gave Willy some fine new shoes. The baker could not say "No," and he gave Willy some bread to eat.

As Willy was walking down the street, he met the same rich man he had worked for. The rich man was on his way to the bank, and his pockets were full of gold.

"Well, Willy," said the man. "What fine clothes you have!"

"Oh, my clothes are not so fine as my fiddle," said Willy. "My fiddle makes everyone who hears it dance."

"Then sometime I should like to hear you play it," laughed the rich man.

"Another wonderful thing has happened to me," said Willy. "No one can say 'No' to anything I ask. Do you see the apples on that tree over there? If I should ask you to get one for me, you could not say 'No' to me."

The rich man did not believe Willy. He thought that he was just telling a silly tale.

"If you can do that, I will give you all the gold in my pockets," he said.

But when Willy asked the man to get an apple, he could not say "No" and started toward the tree.

As the man walked through some bushes, they scratched him and tore his jacket. They even tore his cap. By the time an apple was in his hand, his clothes were in rags.

When he looked at his torn clothes, the rich man became very, very angry with Willy. When he had to give Willy all of his gold, he became even angrier.

The rich man was so angry that he went to see the watchman at the town hall. He told the watchman that Willy had taken his fiddle and all of his gold.

At once the watchman went running to catch Willy. Everyone in the town hall went running after the watchman to see what would happen.

When Willy saw the rich man and the watchman, leading all the people toward him, he began to play his fiddle. As soon as the watchman heard the music he began to dance. The rich man heard the music, and he began to dance, too.

All the people stopped running and started to dance. Even the dogs and cats, horses and cows, began to dance.

Willy played his fiddle for a long time. When he stopped, everyone was so tired that they had to go home to rest. Even the watchman and the rich man went home without harming Willy.

So away Willy went. Everywhere he went, he had good luck because he had his fine fiddle and because no one could ever say "No" to him.

Norse Folk Tale

The Fairy Book

When Mother takes the Fairy Book
    And we curl up to hear,
'Tis "All aboard for Fairyland!"
    Which seems to be so near.

For soon we reach the pleasant place
    Of Once Upon a Time,
Where birdies sing the hour of day,
    And flowers talk in rhyme;

Where Little People live in nuts,
    And ride on butterflies,
And wonders kindly come to pass
    Before your very eyes.

It is the nicest time of day
    Though bedtime is so near,—
When Mother takes the Fairy Book
    And we curl up to hear.

Abbie Farwell Brown

Players of All Kinds

The people of Timber Town liked to see and hear players and singers. So, many bands and orchestras came to their town. Even the children planned music programs and plays.

Here are some stories about players of Timber Town and players of long ago.

Charlie and the Whistle

The Merry Music Makers' Club, of which Jan was a member, planned a program for their parents and friends.

At first there was to be only band music. Then Mr. Rock, the teacher, thought it would be nice to sing, too.

Pete Young had another idea. "Why can't we whistle a song like 'Our Flag'?" he asked.

"That's a fine idea, Pete," said Mr. Rock. "Every boy likes to whistle."

Now, Charlie Day was in the club, and he could not whistle. He had often tried, but the whistle never came through.

The next morning, Charlie sat on his front porch. He was unhappy because he could not whistle. He had to think of another idea, or he could not be in the show.

Charlie's dog Inky came over and sat near him. Inky knew Charlie was not happy.

"Good old Inky," Charlie said. "You don't care if I can't whistle."

Later, Charlie heard someone coming up the street whistling. It was Pete Young and some other members of the club.

"Hi, Charlie!" shouted Pete. "We are on our way to work on our program. Have you learned to whistle yet?"

"No," answered Charlie, "but I have an idea. Couldn't I be the leader of the whistling band? Then I wouldn't have to whistle. I could just wave my arms."

"Nothing doing!" said Frank, the older boy. "You can't rob me of my job."

"Well, that's out," said Charlie to his dog as the boys walked away. Then he took some money from his pocket. "I might just as well use this twenty-five cents for a chocolate milk shake. Maybe that will make me feel better," he said.

Charlie got on his bicycle and rode off to Mr. Simon's shop. He was just about to ask for the chocolate milk shake when he saw a big sign that said, "Whistles, Twenty-five Cents."

Charlie went over and looked at the strange-looking long whistles.

"Oh, are these real whistles?" Charlie asked Mr. Simon.

"That's what they are," replied Mr. Simon. "Some people call them flutes, but they are just whistles, that's all."

Mr. Simon picked up a whistle and played it.

"Say, that's just what I need!" cried Charlie. "Do you think that I could learn to play it in a day or two?"

"There's nothing to it," laughed Mr. Simon. He showed Charlie how to play a tune on the little flute.

All that afternoon, Charlie sat on his porch and tried one tune after another. All the while, Inky put his head back and cried, "Owoo, owoo, owoo!"

"What on earth are you doing to that dog?" Charlie's mother called out.

Charlie pushed Inky away and began to play again. Inky scampered right back and cried, "Owoo!"

Their neighbor looked out the window and shouted, "Leave that poor dog alone!"

So Charlie put Inky in his bedroom and closed the door. Then he ran down to Pete's house.

"Have you learned to whistle yet?" Pete asked.

"Yes, listen to this," replied Charlie, and he began to play a tune.

"That's great, Charlie!" cried the boys —all but Frank, who thought the whistle was too loud to use in the program.

"It is so loud that it would be the only whistle that you could hear," he said.

The other boys knew Frank was right.

"Why don't you play a tune all by yourself?" asked David.

"Yes, that's a good idea," said the other boys.

Mr. Rock thought it was a fine idea, too. So Charlie was allowed to be in the program.

At last, Wednesday evening came. The children were all dressed up for the program. The hall was filled with people. First, all the boys and girls in the club sang a song. Then the band played.

"Now we have a surprise for you," Mr. Rock told the people. "Charlie Day will play the flute."

Charlie came out. His face was red. He felt warm and excited.

As he started to play, a sound came from outside. It sounded like five dogs having red-hot pins put into them.

"Owoo, owoo, owoo!" It was Inky.

Charlie stopped playing. "I'm afraid that's my dog," he said to Mr. Rock.

Everyone in the hall laughed and clapped.

"Bring the dog in," Mr. Rock told the boys.

As soon as the door was opened, Inky scampered inside and right up to Charlie. As Charlie played, Inky cried, "Owoo, owoo, owoo!" Again the people laughed and clapped.

Soon it was time for the other boys to whistle the tune to "Our Flag," but they were all so tickled and were laughing so hard that no one could whistle.

"I'm sorry about my dog doing that to your part of the program," Charlie told Frank and the other boys later.

"Oh, that's all right," Frank replied. "Even the monkeys and clowns at the circus are not as funny as that was. Just tell us where you got that flute or whistle or whatever it is so that we can teach our dogs to sing, too."

The next day, Mr. Simon had to take the Twenty-five Cent sign down. All his flutes were gone.

Eleanor Clymer

The Toy Orchestra

"Have you heard the good news?" Peter asked Matt early one morning.

"What news?" asked Matt.

"About the new children's playhouse," answered his friend. "My parents told me about it last night. They said that Father Michaels wants all of us to join it during the next few months."

"Who wants to play house?" laughed Matt. "That's all right for Peggy and Melissa and the girls but not for us."

"You're all wrong on that," replied Peter. "You don't have the right idea. The playhouse is like a theater, just for children, where we can put on plays."

"Oh, that's different," said Matt. "You mean we would be allowed to make up the plays and be in them?"

"Yes," answered Peter. "Miss Karen will help us."

Before the month was over, most of the Timber Town families had heard about the children's new theater. Peter, Matt, Peggy, Melissa, and many others were already members.

The children were busy as bees, and by the end of the month they were ready to give their first play. It was about the first toy orchestra and the man who started it.

Toy Orchestra Players

JOSEPH HAYDN	FATHER HAYDN
FARMER	BAND PLALYERS
COUSIN FRANK	JIM
MOTHER HAYDN	STORYTELLER

ORCHESTRA PLAYERS

Part I

TIME. Early morning, many years ago.

PLACE. The market place of a small village in a far-off country across the sea.

JOSEPH HAYDN (*hurrying into the market place*). Everyone in our house is still sleeping, but I heard the farmers' wagons going by. I must hurry if I want to see all the good things they are bringing for market day.

FARMER (*standing near the market place*). Hello, there, Joseph! Do you always get up with the sun? Come over here and have some breakfast with me. (*He hands Joseph an apple.*)

JOSEPH HAYDN. This is going to be a wonderful day for me. My cousin Frank is coming to visit us today. You should hear him play the violin! Perhaps he is already at our house. I must run home and see.

STORYTELLER. As Joseph Haydn ran down the road toward his home, he saw his cousin going into the yard. Frank was carrying a violin under his arm.

JOSEPH HAYDN. Hello, Cousin Frank, hello! Will you please play your violin for me right now? Will you teach me to play it, too?

COUSIN FRANK *(showing the violin to Joseph)*. A violin is very hard to play, Joseph. You are too young to learn now. Perhaps when you are a little older, your parents can send you to live with me. Then I shall teach you to sing and to play the violin and other things in a big orchestra.

MOTHER HAYDN *(greeting Frank)*. We are so glad you have come, Cousin Frank. For weeks, Joseph has talked of nothing else. He wants so much to hear you play your violin.

FATHER HAYDN. He thinks of nothing but music. He sits for hours at a time, singing songs and playing with two pieces of wood which he calls his violin.

Part II

TIME. One year later.

PLACE. Cousin Frank's home.

COUSIN FRANK. Joseph! Joseph! Can you play a drum?

JOSEPH HAYDN *(putting his violin down excitedly)*. No, but if you will teach me, I'm sure that I can play it.

COUSIN FRANK *(playing a tune on a make-believe drum)*. If you can learn quickly, you can play in the big parade this afternoon. The drummer is ill, and there isn't anyone else in the band who can take his place.

JOSEPH HAYDN *(playing hard on the drum)*. One, two, three, rest!

COUSIN FRANK. That's fine, Joseph! Come now, and you shall see the real drum you are to play in the parade. *(He leads Joseph into a room where the band players are getting ready for the big parade.)*

JOSEPH HAYDN *(looking at the very large drum).* That is a wonderful drum, but how can I carry it?

ONE OF THE BAND PLAYERS. Put the drum on my back, Frank. If you put it low enough, Joseph can walk behind me and hit it as I walk in front of him.

STORYTELLER. Frank put the large drum on the back of the band player, but still it was not low enough for Joseph to reach.

COUSIN FRANK *(calling a shorter man).* Jim will be glad to carry the drum on his back. Jim has always wanted to be in a parade. Now he can be in one without having to play in the band.

STORYTELLER. So Jim carried the drum on his strong back, and Joseph Haydn walked behind, playing it as the parade marched through the village streets.

Before Joseph was nine years old, he could play and sing very well. His voice was like an angel's from heaven.

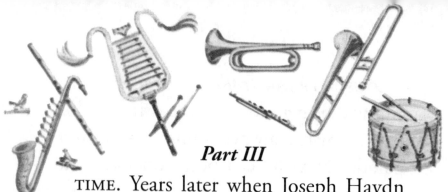

Part III

TIME. Years later when Joseph Haydn was a man.

PLACE. The village in which Haydn was born.

JOSEPH HAYDN *(standing before the shop window of a music store).* Those are toy music-makers. Let me see, there are drums, horns, bells, woodwinds, and bird whistles. I think I shall buy enough to have a toy orchestra for my men. *(He goes into store and buys the toys.)*

STORYTELLER. Now, the men in Haydn's orchestra were all wonderful players, and they played music that all the world loved to hear. Before Joseph Haydn took his toy music-makers to the men, he wrote a lovely tune for a toy orchestra.

JOSEPH HAYDN. Now my men can play this music with their toys. We will have the first toy orchestra in the world!

STORYTELLER. At first, the men were angry with Joseph Haydn for playing a trick on them, but before long they were having a good time playing the lovely music he had made for them. From that time to this, people all over the world have learned about the toy orchestra. Almost every school has a toy orchestra or a toy band for young children who are too small to play in a real school band or orchestra.

Opal Wheeler and Sybil Deucher

Francis and the Concert

"Oh, boy! Hot dogs for supper," said Francis Hunt, reaching across the table for the dish of hot dogs.

"Watch your manners, young man," said his father. "Table manners are just as important with hot dogs as they are when we have chocolate ice cream and cake or cherry pie."

Francis pushed the dish back. He made the Sign of the Cross and said the prayer before meals with the rest of the family. As he finished, he turned to his mother.

"This is great, Mother," he said. "Why don't we have this kind of meal every Monday night?"

"I'm glad you like hot dogs so well," replied Mrs. Hunt. "I really just wanted to have something that would be quick and easy to fix."

"Well, Francis," said his older sister, Bernadette, "you had better hurry with that dish of hot dogs, or we will all be late for the band concert."

"Band concert!" gasped Francis. "You mean a band concert with music?"

Mr. Hunt smiled. "I'm sure I don't know what else a band concert could have if it did not have music, do you?"

"Oh, Dad, we are not just going to sit and listen to music all evening, are we?" said Francis.

"You might learn to like it if you would sit still long enough to listen," said Bernadette.

"That will do, children," said Mr. Hunt. "Talking will not help us to get to the concert on time."

Francis was very quiet through the rest of the meal. A band concert! The very thought of it changed the taste of his hot dog. It didn't even taste good to him any more.

The Hunt family got to the park by half-past seven. Francis was surprised to see his friend Matt Lake there. The two families found places together. Matt and Melissa sat next to Francis.

Some of the band players, dressed in bright red coats, were already in the bandstand. They were getting their horns, flutes, and drums in tune. The sound was terrible, but it didn't last long.

In a few minutes, the band leader raised his hand. The people in the park became quiet, and the music began.

Francis had been talking to Matt about a ball game he had seen on TV. He wanted to keep on, but Matt did not seem to want to talk. He was looking toward the bandstand, listening to the music.

Francis looked up at the sky to see if he could find the evening star. "I know what I will wish on that star this evening," he said in a low voice. "No more band concerts!"

After a while, Francis was surprised to see that his foot was moving up and down with the music. "Those horns are pretty good," he said to himself.

Francis watched the drummers as they started playing their drums. He had fun trying to move his foot every time the drummers hit the drums. He was keeping time with the music.

"Say, this is fun!" he said quietly.

Suddenly the concert stopped, and the band leader began to speak to the people. He had a surprise for the children.

Soon all the children in the park were marching around the bandstand to the tune of "The March of the Wooden Soldiers."

Around and around they went, Francis, Matt, Peggy, Melissa, and many other Timber Town children. They all laughed as they kept in step with the music.

After the concert was over, the Lakes and the Hunts went home.

Francis didn't say much about the concert until the next Monday evening when he called into the house, "Say, Mother, we're having hot dogs for dinner, aren't we? We don't want to be late for the concert."

Mary A. Goulding

Drum Music

Some music is to hear,
Some music is to sing;
And some is dancing music
Like bells and birds in spring.

But drums make marching music
With their beat, beat, beat.
Drum music is the kind
That gets into your feet.

Hazel G. Kinscella

The Little Music-Maker

It was a lovely warm summer evening in a small village far across the sea. The sun was beginning to go behind the clouds in the west, and a cool breeze began to blow over the village. The evening star could be seen shining brightly over the home of the village shoemaker.

Music filled the air. The shoemaker's son was playing his violin. It was the only thing the young boy had, and he treasured it dearly.

The shoemaker sat in the doorway of his small home and listened for a long time to his son play the beautiful music.

Then the old man said sadly, "Son, if only you could earn some money with that violin!

"You play well, but we are poor people who need food. Perhaps you had better sell the violin, my boy, and find yourself a good job."

Mark stopped playing and looked up. His father could no longer do much work because he was ill.

"If that is what you want, Father," he said, "of course, I will do it. But first, I will try to earn money without selling the violin.

"Tomorrow I shall go to the village hall and play for the people as they walk by. If my music pleases them, surely they will offer me a few cents, and then we may buy some food."

The shoemaker thought the boy's idea was good enough to try. So the next day Mark sat on the steps of the village hall and played his violin.

He had been there for only a little while when a company of singers came along. They were surprised to find a young boy who could play so well.

"We go from town to town singing our songs," they told Mark. "If you come with us, you will earn much money and become a rich man some day."

Mark was happy to hear the good news and hurried home to tell his father about his new job.

"You may go with the company of singers, my son," said the shoemaker, "but don't stay away for long. You are all I have, and I shall miss you very much."

"As soon as I have enough money to take you to a good doctor, I shall come back," said the boy.,

The singers who had promised Mark so much money did not keep their word. They made him work hard, but they did not give him any money.

Three years passed by, and still the boy had no money to send home to his poor ill father.

One summer day, the singers went into a small town named after our Blessed Mother. Mark remembered that it was one of her great feast days.

"Let's go over to the Catholic church this evening," Mark said to the men. "All the people in town will be there because this is a great feast day. We can earn money by playing and singing in front of the crowd."

"You may go there by yourself if you wish," the leader told Mark. "There are other places where we can make money."

That evening, when the church bell started ringing, Mark took his violin and hurried off to St. Mary's Church.

When the boy went inside, he forgot all about earning money. The church was crowded with people who were all praying the Rosary together.

Soon young Mark, too, was whispering, "Holy Mary, Mother of God, pray for us sinners, now and at the hour of our death. Amen."

It was late before everyone had left the church, and Mark was all alone.

In the dark, Mark could just see Mary's altar. He could see the beautiful flowers in front of it. He walked quietly up to the altar. There he began to play a lovely song to Our Lady.

The pastor heard the music and came into the church to see who was playing.

"Who's there? Who's there?" called out the pastor.

Mark felt frightened, and he began to hurry away. Because he could not see well in the dark church, he ran right into the arms of the good priest.

Surely that must have been just what our Blessed Lady wanted, for from that night on, Mark and the priest became very good friends.

When the kind pastor heard about the boy's poor sick father, he took Mark back to him. Then he found a doctor to take care of the shoemaker. He also made plans for the little violin player to go to a fine music school in a large city.

As the years passed, Mark became a great violin player. He played in cities and towns and countries all over the world. Every day he found time to go to Mass and thank our Blessed Lady for the way in which she had helped him.

Jenny the Nightingale

"Look, James," cried Marie, as she held up the morning newspaper. "Here is a picture of Jenny Lind."

Jenny Lind was a singer who lived years ago in a country across the sea.

"She is coming to this country next week and right here to our 'own city,'" said Marie. "My music teacher said she has a voice like a nightingale."

James, Marie's brother, looked up from a bird that he was making from a piece of wood. "Does Jenny Lind sing better than you?" he asked his sister.

James thought that Marie had a voice like a bird's. And James loved birds. He read books about them and painted pictures of them. He even made many different kinds of birds from wood.

"Don't be silly," laughed Marie. "I'll never sing like Jenny Lind."

"Where will Jenny Lind sing when she comes to our city?" Marie's brother asked. "I've been saving my money, and I already have eighty cents, which I can give you if you want to buy a ticket."

Marie smiled and said, "Miss Lind will sing at the Music Hall. The seats are eight dollars each. Standing space is two dollars, and it costs one dollar just to get a place on the roof."

Marie went on, "I can't ask Father for that much money. He is already paying a dollar a week for my singing lessons."

James looked at his sister. "I know a place where there are a lot of blackberry bushes," he said. "Perhaps we could pick enough to buy a standing ticket if I add my eighty cents."

Marie clapped her hands. "That's a wonderful idea!" she cried, "but I don't want to use your eighty cents. You were saving that to buy a new knife."

"I can buy a knife any time," replied James, "but this may be the only time Jenny Lind ever comes to America."

The next morning, Marie and James set out for the blackberry patch. All day long they worked until their pails were filled. They were very tired.

Just as they started down the hill to go home, Marie turned her foot on a stone and fell down.

"Oh, look out for the blackberries!" she cried.

James picked up the pail. Only a few berries had fallen out. "Are you hurt?" he asked his sister. "You are a lot more important than the blackberries."

"Not a lot more important than these berries," Marie said. "These are special Jenny-Lind-ticket berries."

She stood up and tried to walk. "I guess I'm all right," she said.

Marie's foot was badly hurt. By the time she got home, it hurt so much that she could not even stand on it. Her mother called the doctor.

"Your daughter will have to stay off that foot for a week or ten days," the doctor told Marie's mother.

Marie felt terrible. "What good is a standing ticket at the Music Hall if I can't stand?" she said.

"You must go to hear Jenny Lind," Marie told her brother. "You can tell me if her voice is really like a nightingale's."

"How can I even tell that about Jenny Lind's singing?" replied James. "I've never heard a nightingale sing."

Marie laughed. "Then you can tell me if Jenny Lind's voice is as sweet as a jenny wren's, like the one that nests out in our apple tree," she said.

The next few days went by very slowly for Marie. James tried to buy a ticket with the money he got for the berries.

"Sorry," said the ticket man. "There is nothing left but roof space, and the police will not allow young boys up there."

Then James thought of a secret plan. On the morning when Jenny Lind came to the city, he ate breakfast very fast. He put something in his coat pocket and hurried to the building where Miss Lind was staying.

"I have a gift for Miss Lind," James told the elevator man, so he was allowed to go up.

As James stepped out of the elevator, he saw all kinds of important people standing near Jenny Lind's room. They were all waiting to see her. He wondered if he would really be allowed to see the great singer.

Then at last his turn came. The door opened, and James found himself inside the room with Jenny Lind.

"What can I do for you, young man?" Miss Lind asked in a kind manner.

James felt braver when he heard her voice. "I've brought a little gift for you, and I have a favor to ask," he answered. Then he reached into his pocket and pulled out a little jenny wren that he had made from wood.

"This is an American nightingale," he said. "I made this one just for you."

Miss Lind looked at the little wooden wren. "How lovely this is!" she said. "Because you made it by yourself, I shall always keep it as a treasure. Now, what is the favor, young man?"

The singer's smile was so kind and warm that James almost forgot that he was speaking to a very important lady. He told her all about his sister Marie.

"I was wondering," James said, "if you would come to our house and sing just one little song for my sister."

At once, Miss Lind got her coat and went with James to his house.

No girl ever had a more wonderful surprise than Marie had that day. Her eyes almost jumped out of her head when the door opened and she saw her brother leading the great singer into the house.

Jenny Lind shook hands with Marie. Then she sang one beautiful song after another as sweetly as a nightingale.

When Marie tried to thank the singer, Miss Lind said, "You must thank your brother. It was he who made a little jenny wren for me. I shall always keep it to remember you and your country."

Helen Reeder Cross

Rumpelstiltskin

Here is the last play the children of Timber Town gave in their own theater during the month of March.

RUMPELSTILTSKIN PLAYERS

Moonlight	King
Sunlight	Maybell
Starlight	Maid
Rumpelstiltskin	

Part I

TIME. Early Morning.

PLACE. A large room in the king's place where three servant girls are cleaning/

MOONLIGHT *(dusting off a chair).* Just think! The king has asked a very poor miller's daughter to come to the palace!

SUNLIGHT. Is that why we have all this cleaning to do before the sun sets?

STARLIGHT. Yes, It is. I saw the miller's daughter in front of the palace the other day.

MOONLIGHT. Is she as beautiful as the king says?

STARLIGHT. Yes, Maybell is the prettiest young girl I have ever seen.

SUNLIGHT. She may have a beautiful face, but she's a lazy good-for-nothing. That is what I heard from the old woman who goes to market every week. On her way there she passes the miller's house by the river, so she knows about Maybell.

MOONLIGHT. Maybell's father must not think she is lazy. He told the king that she spins all day long, and that she is clever enough to spin straw into gold.

SUNLIGHT. How can anyone spin straw into gold? The miller was talking out of his head.

STARLIGHT. Quiet! Here comes the king, and he has the miller's clever daughter with him. Look, she is dressed in rags.

KING *(looking at the servants).* Where is the straw? We need a large pile of it. Be off, and get it at once!

SERVANTS *(bowing before the king). We* go at once, your Majesty!

KING. Well, my dear Maybell, this is the room in which you will work.

MAYBELL. Your Majesty, my father told you that I can spin straw into gold, but it is not true. I can never do that. Please let me go home.

KING. Don't try to get out of this now, my dear Maybell. Straw into gold! Ah, I can hardly wait to see it!

SERVANTS *(carrying large piles of straw into the room)*. Here is the straw, your Majesty.

KING. Now be off to your work at once! Tomorrow you shall see this room filled with gold.

MAYBELL *(looking sadly at the king)*. Your Majesty, what will happen if this straw is not turned to gold by tomorrow?

KING. Your father will be punished for telling something that is not true.

MAYBELL *(crying and falling on her knees)*. My poor father! Oh, please do not do anything to him, your Majesty!

KING *(leaving the room)*. Should this straw be changed into gold, you shall do me the favor of becoming my wife. You shall be queen of all my land. Good-night, fair lady. Begin your work!

MAYBELL *(suddenly surprised by a wee, strange man).* Who are you?

RUMPELSTILTSKIN *(jumping about the* room). Never mind who. I know you. You live where the river runs by. Why, oh, why do you cry?

MAYBELL. My father did something terrible. He told the king that I can spin straw into gold, and I do not know how to do it.

RUMPELSTILTSKIN. What will you give me if I turn this straw into gold?

MAYBELL *(holding out her hand).* The ring from my finger!

RUMPELSTILTSKIN. This straw is very poor stuff. Your ring will not be enough.

MAYBELL. What else have I to offer?

RUMPELSTILTSKIN. Gold from this straw I will make. And your first child I will take.

MAYBELL. I'll promise you my first child. The king will never really want a miller's daughter for his wife anyway.

RUMPELSTILTSKIN *(twisting and spinning around).* Maybell, sit and watch me spin, so the king's heart you can win. Straw to gold, and gold to crown, before the sun's next going down.

Part II

TIME. One year later.

PLACE. Queen's bedroom. Maybell is dressed as a queen and is watching over her baby.

MAID *(coming into the room)*. Your Majesty, I'm afraid to leave you here alone. What if that terrible little man should come back and make you keep your promise!

MAYBELL. Oh, dear! I don't even want to think of him. Yet, he did help me to spin the straw into gold.

MAID. He will let you keep your baby if you can guess his name.

MAYBELL. My servants have guessed. I have guessed. Every name is wrong. Today he will come, and this will be the last time I can try to guess his name.

MAID. If only something could be done!

MOONLIGHT (*gasping and running in with Sunlight and Starlight. They have run so fast that they can hardly talk.*) Oh, your Majesty! This morning, we went into the woods. We climbed a high hill and saw something.

SUNLIGHT. A tiny house with a fire in front of it!

STARLIGHT. And dancing around the fire was a little elf-like man, singing a strange song and brewing something.

THREE SERVANTS *(singing together)*. Today I bake, tomorrow I brew. Glad I am that no one knew Rumpelstiltskin is my name. Now the queen's child I can claim.

MAYBELL. Ah! So it's Rumpelstiltskin! You have done well. Go now! Here comes the little man.

RUMPELSTILTSKIN *(singing and rubbing his hands as he comes in)*. Today I bake, tomorrow I brew. Good, evening, my Maybell, fair and proud. This is the last guess you'll be allowed.

MAYBELL. Is your name Tom?

RUMPELSTILTSKIN. No! Ah, no!

MAYBELL. Could it be Whistle Breeze?

RUMPELSTILTSKIN. No! No! Ah, no!

MAYBELL. Well, let me see! Can your name be Rumpelstiltskin?

RUMPELSTILTSKIN *(jumping up and down and looking very angry because now he cannot claim the queen's child).* Some old witch, some old witch, some old witch has told you! *(He stamps out of the room. The three little servants and the maid come in.)*

ALL *(singing and dancing together).*

We wish you good evening,
Mr. Rumpelstiltskin.
We wish you good feasting,
Mr. Rumpelstiltskin.
A happy queen and very fine weather!
In happiness we all dance together.

Wilhelm and Jacob Grimm

Young Citizens of Timber Town

Boys and girls of Timber Town worked hard to make their town a better place in which to live. Each one tried to do his part. They did this all the time, but these stories show how they worked even harder in April.

Saint Francis and the Wolf

One lovely day, Father Michaels was taking all of the altar boys from his church to Crown Park for a picnic.

The bus that was to take them there was late. So Father Michaels told the boys this story while they waited.

In a country far away, there once lived a holy man named Francis. He was so good and so kind that everyone called him a saint.

Saint Francis loved everybody. He loved all the birds and the animals too. He even called the chipmunks and wild bunnies his little sisters and brothers because they came from God, the Father of us all.

Now, in a village near the city where Francis lived, there was a large wolf. All the people in that village and the country about were afraid of the wolf, for he had done many terrible things.

Stories were often told how the wolf had carried away children. When farm animals and even people were missing, everybody knew that the wolf had been out again.

People were afraid to go very far away from their homes, for the wolf lived near the walls of the village.

Brave men had often gone out to hunt for the wolf and kill him, but they could never find him.

One day, some of the people heard about
Francis and the wonderful things he could
do with animals. They heard that the saint
loved animals, and that all the animals
seemed to love him, too. They thought
that perhaps Francis could tame the
terrible wolf.

Some of the men went to see Francis.
They asked him to come and help them.

"I will go to the wolf and ask him what
he means," said Francis.

"He will kill you! He will eat you up!"
gasped the men.

"There is something good in everything that God has made," said the gentle saint. "Perhaps with a little kindness, we can tame even this terrible wolf."

So Saint Francis started out toward the walls of the village. Large crowds of people followed him to see what would happen.

Soon the wolf came rushing down from the hills.

The people became so frightened that they all ran away and left Francis alone. They stood on a high hill where they could watch and see what the saint would do.

Saint Francis was not afraid. He kept walking toward the wild animal who was rushing straight toward him with hungry-looking eyes.

When the wolf came near enough, Francis made the Sign of the Cross over him. Then the good saint began to speak to the animal.

"Come here, Brother Wolf," he said. "In the name of God, I ask you never again to hurt any of His people."

The wolf walked straight to Saint Francis and lay quietly at his feet. He seemed to like the soft, gentle voice of the saint.

Francis went on, "Brother Wolf, you have done much harm in this part of the country. You have hurt people who, like you, were made by God. I believe you have done this because you were hungry. Is that not so?"

The wolf made a sound as if he were trying to say "Yes."

"Now, Brother Wolf, if you will stop doing harm to God's people, I will see that you get food," Francis said.

"The people of this village will be glad to give you all you can eat, but you must stop hurting them and taking their children and animals."

The wolf put his foot into the hand of the saint as if he were trying to tell him that he would never again do the terrible things he had done in the past.

"Come, Brother Wolf," said Francis. "We will go into the city and show all the people how tame and good you are."

In a little while, the people heard about Francis bringing the wolf into the village.

All of them, young and old, went hurrying out into the streets to see for themselves what was going to happen.

With the terrible wolf walking softly at his side, the saint walked through the village. The wolf now seemed as gentle and tame as a pet dog.

The saint said to the people, "Brother Wolf has promised to do no more harm to anyone. Will you all promise to give him something to eat every day?"

Everybody promised to give the hungry wolf something to eat as long as he lived if only he would leave them alone.

The wolf knelt and put his head down, as if to show that he was sorry for the wrong he had done and that he would keep his promise.

Then the people of the village all cried out and gave thanks to God, Who had sent Saint Francis to them to tame the terrible wolf.

Not long after this, Francis left the village, but the wolf stayed with the people.

Every day the wolf was given something to eat, and he became so tame that he walked in and out of the houses like a pet.

After a few years, the wolf died. The people, who had once been so afraid of him, now missed him, for he had become a gentle friend.

When Father Michaels had finished the story, he said, "Saint Francis was a good citizen, as well as a saint. He helped to make the town a safer place for the people.

"There are many ways in which we, too, can help to make Timber Town a good place in which to live." The priest asked the boys to think of some things they could do at their picnic that day.

"We are going to roast hot dogs at our picnic today," said Matt Lake. "We can put the fire out after we have roasted them."

"Good citizens keep their parks clean," added Peter. "We should put our lunch bags and candy papers into the cans and not leave them around on the ground."

While the boys were talking, a large bus came into the schoolyard. "Hurrah! Hurrah!" cried the excited boys, and they rushed off to their hot dog roast.

Lazy Charlie

The first week in April was called Timber Town Week. During that week, all the grownups worked to make the town a better place in which to live.

"I wish there was something children could do to help," said Melissa Lake to her friend Peggy Martin as they walked in the park. "The grownups are doing almost all the work."

"My big brother Bob is on the park committee," said Peggy proudly. "He helped to plant these pretty flowers."

"Here come Matt and Peter," said Melissa. "Maybe they can think of some way that we can help."

"You are right," said Matt as soon as Melissa and Peggy had told the boys what they were thinking.

"We should have a young citizens' committee and do things for our town," said Peter. "Everybody else seems to be on some kind of committee."

"Daddy is on a committee to make our town a safer place," said Peggy.

"My father is on that committee, too," said Matt. "He said they are going to try to get more stop lights on some of the streets."

"I heard Mr. Marks, our neighbor, say that we need better street lights on some of the side streets," said Melissa.

"Here comes Jan," said Peter. "Maybe he can think of what our young citizens' committee can do."

"He has a dog with him," said Peggy. "That's not a dog," said Matt. "It looks more like a calf or a goat."

"A goat!" cried Peter as Jan came nearer. "Where on earth did you get a goat, Jan?"

"Maa-a-a-a!" whined the goat over and over again.

"My uncle who lives on a farm promised to give me a pet when I was old enough to take care of one," explained Jan. "Last night, he came to our house with Charlie."

"Maa-a-a-a!" whined Charlie again. He began to eat the leaves of one of the new bushes that had just been planted in the park.

It took all five children to pull Charlie away from the bush.

"We need a committee just to take care of Charlie," laughed Peter. "There will not be any leaves left on the bushes around here if he keeps on eating them."

"I have an idea for our young citizens' committee!" cried Matt. "Let's have a clean-up committee and put Charlie on it. We'll go around and pick up trash in the park and on the sidewalks. Charlie can help us to take the trash away."

"We can use my wagon," said Peter. "We'll pile the trash in the wagon, and Charlie can pull it."

Jan said, "It will make Charlie feel very proud to be on the young citizens' committee."

Peter ran home and got his wagon and some rope.

"This rope is for you, Charlie," Peter explained to the goat after he came back. "The rope will help you pull the wagon. You are going to be a busy goat."

Peter tied the rope to Charlie. Then Peter and Jan tied the rope to the wagon. Charlie shook his head very hard. Then in a loud, angry voice he cried, "Maa-a-a-a-a!"

"I don't think he wants to be on the young citizens' committee," laughed Melissa.

"He'll be all right when he gets used to the rope," said Jan.

Charlie would not pull the wagon. He just stood very still.

"Charlie, you are not a good citizen of Timber Town. You are lazy, very lazy," Jan said to his pet.

It took all five children to make Charlie move. They pulled and pushed him. Finally Charlie pulled the wagon.

"Look, there's some trash over there," said Melissa.

The children left Charlie and started picking up some papers on the grass. Some other boys and girls came by and joined the young citizens' committee. Everyone was busy picking up papers.

They didn't see what Charlie was doing, until Melissa cried, "Jan, come and help me."

Charlie was busy eating the tops off the flowers that had just been planted in the park.

Jan caught the rope that was tied to Charlie's neck and tried to pull the goat away from the flowers.

"Pulling Charlie is harder than trying to pull an oak tree out of the ground," Jan said to Melissa who was trying to help him.

"Help us," Jan cried to the other children.

It took nearly all of the children to pull
Charlie away from the flowers. Only Peter
was picking up trash.

When he came over to put some trash
into the wagon, he laughed. "It takes a
committee just to take care of Charlie. We
could do more work without him," Peter
said.

"If we could just take him away from
these flowers, maybe we could get some
work done," said Jan.

It took so much pulling to get Charlie
out on the sidewalk, that the young
citizens' committee had to sit down to rest.
While they were resting, Charlie was doing
something else.

"Oh, please get that goat away from my
bushes," cried a woman from her house.

The children jumped up and pulled and
pulled at the rope tied to Charlie's neck.
Finally he moved away from the bushes.
This time the children pulled Charlie all
the way back to Jan's house and tied him
in the backyard.

Charlie looked unhappy because he was tied. He disliked a rope or anything on his neck.

"Poor Charlie," said Jan, "you are not a city pet. Tomorrow, we'll take you back to the farm to your other animal friends. We can come to visit you there."

"Maa-a-a-a!" Charlie whined in a happy way.

The young citizens went back to work. This time they took turns pulling the wagon, and they got much more work done without lazy Charlie.

Things Happen in Frog Corners

Jean Miller, Patty Fields, and Billy Fox lived in Frog Corners, a small village just outside of Timber Town.

Patty and Billy went to the River Street School. Jean went to St. Francis School.

The road on which the children lived was not paved, and they had a hard time trying to keep their shoes clean. When it rained, Bean Road was wet and muddy. In the summertime, it was dry and dusty.

One day after they had finished their lessons, the children in Jean's class talked about ways to make Timber Town a better place.

As the children talked, Jean wondered what she could say. "Frog Corners really does not belong to Timber Town," she explained to the class, "but I wish that we could do something to make our village a nicer place, too."

"You can obey the leaders of your village," said one of the boys.

"You can help to keep the streets clean," said another.

Jean smiled. "I wish we knew how to keep Bean Road clean," she said. "It is not a paved street, and if it is not muddy, it is dry and dusty."

That evening after school, Jean, Billy, and Patty were telling each other what they had heard in their classes about clean-up week in Timber Town.

"Why don't we try to do something right here in Frog Corners?" said Billy. "Just look at our fences." He pointed to the fences along the road.

"Let's paint them," said Patty. "I'm sure my father will let me have some paint."

"That's a great idea!" cried Billy. After a few minutes Patty was back with a can of paint.

First the children painted Patty's fence green. It was a small fence and did not take long. Then they started painting Jean Miller's fence yellow. Mr. Miller helped the children.

"Tomorrow, we'll help you to paint your fence, Billy," Mr. Miller said.

Late the next day, Mr. Gabriel, one of the neighbors, went out to his mailbox to get the mail. When he saw how nice Patty's, Billy's, and Jean's fences looked, he felt ashamed of his own.

"I'll paint my fence before I do another thing," he said to himself.

Then one neighbor after another began to paint his own fence. Before the end of the week, every fence on Bean Road was a bright, pretty color.

Some of the women planted pretty flowers beside the newly painted fences. The bright fences and the colorful flowers made the people in Frog Corners feel happier.

Then one day Mr. Miller said to Mr. Fields, "The fences look so nice that they make our houses look old and dusty. I really feel ashamed of the way my house looks."

"Yes, I am ashamed of my house, too," said Mr. Fields. "It looks terrible. It needs to be painted and the roof needs to be fixed."

"Mine does, too," said another neighbor.

For the next few evenings, all the men on Bean Road were busy painting and working on their houses.

Before the end of April, all the houses on Bean Road looked so clean and pretty that everybody else in Frog Corners began to work on their homes and yards.

Then something happened to make Jean, Patty, and Billy very happy.

The grownups of Frog Corners joined a citizens' committee. They were trying to get Bean Road paved. Then they could keep Frog Corners clean.

They had long meetings almost every night. Then finally workmen came to Frog Corners and paved Bean Road.

"Now our fences and houses will stay clean," said Patty.

"No more mud on our shoes!" cried Billy.

"No more terrible dry dust on the fences!" cried Jean.

That summer people from other towns and cities flocked to Frog Corners.

"It is one of the prettiest little villages in the country," some of them said.

"And just think!" said the grownups in Frog Corners. "The children started it all."

The Lost Skates

One afternoon, Jan was sitting on the front porch, thinking about his lost skates. He was thinking about them because down the street near the corner, a little boy was skating.

The boy at the corner skated very slowly. Every now and then he fell down. He seemed to be just learning to skate.

When he skated past Jan's house, Jan could tell that the boy's skates were very new.

"They are very much like mine," Jan thought.

The boy skated by again. "They are just like mine," Jan thought.

Then when the boy skated past again, Jan saw on the straps the word *Jan*.

"Why, they are my skates!" he shouted. Jan ran to the sidewalk and stepped out in front of the boy.

"Where did you get my skates?" Jan asked the boy quickly.

The little boy looked up at Jan with round, frightened eyes. "They are not your skates," he said. "They are no one's. The trash man gave them to me this morning."

"I don't care who gave them to you," said Jan crossly. "They are mine. Your name is not Jan, is it?"

The boy shook his head slowly.

"What is your name?" Jan asked.

"My name is Louis," said the boy.

"Well, that shows that the skates are mine. My name is Jan, and here it is," Jan said, pointing to his name on the straps, "right on the straps where I wrote it. So, you see, the skates are mine."

The little boy looked worried and said, "The trash man gave them to me. He said he found them on the side of the street where they had been thrown away."

"They must have rolled out into the street when I took them off," Jan said.

Jan remembered the day last week when he had fallen and hurt his arm. He had taken his skates off and run into his house. When he came back, the skates were not there.

"Well, anyway," he said to Louis, "I didn't throw my skates away. So they are still mine."

"I guess you are right," Louis said slowly. "They must be yours." He took off the skates.

Jan took the skates and ran home. He was happy to have his skates back again. He had spent all week hunting for them.

As soon as Jan got to his doorstep, he looked back. Louis was still sitting where Jan had left him, but the little boy had his head on his arms, and he seemed to be crying.

Later that day, Jan was not so happy about finding his lost skates. He kept thinking about the boy. He remembered seeing Louis sitting on the sidewalk crying, and this did not make Jan happy. His dinner did not even taste good that evening.

Right after Jan had finished his night prayers and said Amen, he made up his mind about what he should do. He went downstairs into the living room where his mother and father were.

"I want to talk to you," Jan said to his parents.

"What is it, son?" his father asked.

Then Jan told them about the boy who had been skating at the corner that afternoon. He told them how the little boy had cried when he took the skates away.

"I think," said Jan at last, "that, if you don't mind, I'll give the skates back to the little boy. He really believed that they were his. Somehow, it doesn't seem right to take them away. After all, the trash man did not know that they were mine."

"I think you are right about that," said his father.

"And I think that you are a very good boy," said his mother as she said good night to Jan.

Mr. Cook found out where Louis lived. The next morning, Jan and his mother went to Louis' house and gave Louis the wonderful skates to keep as his very own. Louis was happy and so was Jan.

While Jan and his mother were going back to their house, Jan suddenly said, "Oh, Mother, I spent so much time yesterday, thinking about the skates, that I forgot to do something for Good Citizens' Week."

"Oh, no, Jan," said his mother, "both yesterday and today you have been kind to your neighbor. That is about the best way to be a good citizen."

Jeannette Covert Nolan

Stars and Stripes
Timber Town Gets a New Flag

Peggy Martin belonged to the Young Citizens' Club. She and some of her friends had a special job in the club. They cut out fifty white stars.

These were very special stars. The club was making a new flag for the town hall. The stars that Peggy helped to cut out were to be sewed on the new flag.

Peggy had another job in the club. She helped to hold the red and white stripes while the older girls sewed them together.

Finally, the club had put together a beautiful flag.

"Hurrah! It's finished! It's finished!" cried Peggy Martin as she rushed into the house late one afternoon.

"What's finished?" asked Mrs. Martin.

"Our new flag," replied Peggy in an excited voice. "Just think, Mother, there were fifty stars to be cut and sewed on the blue field in the corner of the flag!"

"Do you know why there were fifty stars?" Peggy's older brother asked her.

"I suppose so that they would come out even," answered Peggy. "It would not look nice if there were fifty-one stars."

Peggy's big brother laughed when he heard that.

"Those fifty stars mean something important," Bob said. "Each star stands for a state in our country. There are fifty states in all. That is why there are fifty stars in the American flag."

"There were not always fifty states," said Mr. Martin, who had been listening to the children. "At one time, when our country was very young, there were only thirteen states. There is one part of the flag that helps us to remember those first thirteen states. Do you know which part that is?"

Peggy thought for a minute. She was not sure. She went to the table and picked up a small American flag.

Peggy looked at the flag, but the strange look on her face showed that she could not find the part that stood for the first thirteen states.

"Look at the stripes," Mrs. Martin said.

Peggy looked. Then she said, "There are only seven red stripes, and there are only six white stripes."

Her brother laughed a little. "Six and seven are thirteen," he said.

"Oh, now I know," cried Peggy. "The stripes stand for the very first thirteen states."

"That's right," said Mr. Martin as he picked up the evening paper. He began to read, but stopped suddenly.

"Listen to this," he said to Mrs. Martin and the children. Then he began to read out loud.

"The new flag made by the girls in the Young Citizens' Club is to be raised at the town hall on Saturday afternoon," Mr. Martin said.

"That's a big secret," said Peggy in an excited voice. "Yesterday, the big girls in our club told us not to tell."

"It isn't a secret any more," smiled Mrs. Martin. "I suppose the girls did not want to tell until the people read about it in the newspaper."

"Does it tell what we are going to do?" Peggy asked as she looked at her father's newspaper.

Mr. Martin went on reading. "It says that all the citizens of Timber Town are supposed to be there for the flag raising," Mr. Martin said. "It also says that the girls who made the flag will carry it through the streets of the town."

"That's the real secret," cried Peggy. "I'm going to help carry the new flag because I cut out stars and held some of the stripes while the big girls sewed them on the flag."

The Flag Raising

It was Saturday afternoon.

"Rum-a-tum! Rum-a-tum-tum!" went the drums as children in the Young Citizens' Club marched in straight rows down the streets of Timber Town.

The boys played in the band, and the girls marched behind them carrying flags. Last of all came the large flag made by the girls in the club. Thirteen girls, dressed in white, carried that flag.

As the children marched near the town hall, the band began to play.

Crowds of people watched the children as they passed. When they reached the town hall, the band began to play our country's best-loved song, and all the people sang, "Oh, say can you see ...."

Some important men in the town spoke to the people. Mr. Stone from the Timber Town Church was there. He spoke to the people, too.

Finally, Father Michaels blessed the new flag and prayed that God would bless the people of Timber Town.

As the flag was raised, all the people raised their heads and saluted the flag.

The children had saluted the flag many times before, but today the salute had new meaning for them.

"It's great to be an American," said Matt as the three space brothers left the town hall.

The boys turned around to look at the flag again, waving in the bright sunshine. They stood still and gave another salute.

"We have a great country, a great flag, and great people," said Jan.

"We have a great town, too," said Peter. "I'm proud to be an American citizen living in Timber Town."

The Flag

Some flags are red, or white, or green,
And some are yellow, too.
But the dear, dear flag that we love best
Is red, and white, and blue.

We love our native country's flag;
To it our hearts are true.
Above us waves in splendid folds
The red, the white, the blue.

Citizens of Heaven

Some of the boys and girls of Timber Town were getting ready to receive the sacrament of Confirmation. They were reading stories about people who had lived and died for God.

Here are some of the stories that they liked best.

The Child Who Died to Save the Blessed Sacrament

Many, many years ago, there were people who did not know and love God. These people did not want anyone else to love and serve Him. They killed all those who believed in the God of the Christians.

They closed the churches to keep people from going to Mass. But priests offered Mass, and the Christians received Holy Communion in their homes. Sometimes the Christians had to offer the Mass in dimly lighted caves under the ground.

One morning, after a priest had offered the Mass, he looked around the dim cave to find someone to carry the Blessed Sacrament to some of the Christians who were about to die for their faith.

Before anyone had time to go up to the altar to offer help, a young boy named Tarcisius knelt at the priest's feet and held out his hands to take the Blessed Sacrament.

"My boy, you are too young for so dangerous an errand," whispered the priest.

"That is why I should go, Father," said the young boy. "No one will ever think a child is carrying the Heavenly Bread. It will be safe with me. Please do not refuse."

The young boy was so brave that the priest could not refuse his wish. He put the Sacred Host in a fine white cloth. Then he handed It to the child.

"Remember, Tarcisius, what a great Treasure has been put into your care," said the good priest. "Stay away from the crowded places, and keep your Holy Treasure safe."

"Oh, I will die before I let anything happen to It," answered the boy.

He placed the Blessed Sacrament next to his heart and started on his errand.

As Tarcisius hurried along the street, he met a fine lady who had no children of her own.

"Wait a minute, my child," the lady said. "What is your name, and where do you live?"

"I am Tarcisius," replied the boy. "I have no parents. I have no home save one you might not care to hear about."

"Oh, how I wish I had a child like you!" the lady said softly. "Won't you come into my house and visit with me?"

"Thank you, good lady, but I cannot stop today," said Tarcisius. "I am on an errand, and I must hurry."

"Then be sure to come tomorrow. There is my house," she said, pointing to a large white house.

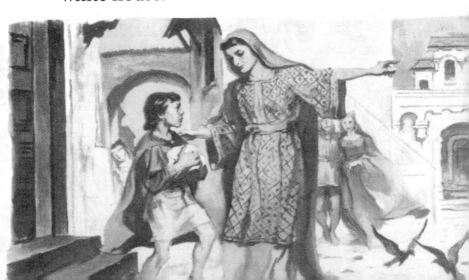

Tarcisius looked at the big, beautiful house longingly. He had always wanted to go into just such a house. He stopped for a moment. Then he thought of his important errand and said, "If I am still alive tomorrow, I will gladly come to your house."

The lady watched Tarcisius as he went down the street. Then she began to follow him. Soon she heard loud cries and screams. She stopped and listened.

In the meantime, Tarcisius had come to a large field where some boys were playing.

"We need one more to make up the game," shouted a big boy. "Here comes Tarcisius, whom I have not seen for a long time. Come, Tarcisius, and take part in our game."

"I cannot play with you now, my friend," answered Tarcisius, "but I shall play some other time."

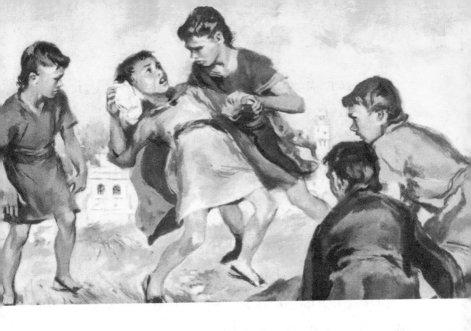

"No, you shall play now," screamed the bossy boy, who was angry because Tarcisius refused to play in the game. The boy took hold of Tarcisius and shook him.

"Please let me go," said the poor child.

"I'll do no such thing. What are you carrying so carefully next to your heart?" asked the angry boy. "A letter? Well, it can wait for half an hour. Give it to me, and I'll keep it for you."

The boy tried to pull the Holy Treasure from Tarcisius.

"Never, never will I give It up," cried Tarcisius.

"I'll see what you have," shouted the boy cruelly. "I will find out what this wonderful secret is."

He beat and hit Tarcisius until the boy fell. Yet, all this time, the young boy kept his hands over his heart.

Soon another voice was heard. "What's wrong?" someone asked.

Then someone else said, "It must be a Christian carrying the Sacrament."

When the crowd heard this, they fell upon poor Tarcisius. They beat him so cruelly that they almost killed him. Still he held his Holy Treasure closely. Suddenly the cruel people felt themselves being pulled away from Tarcisius.

A brave young soldier made his way through the crowd and knelt down beside the child who was almost dead. Tarcisius knew the soldier was a Christian.

"Never mind about me," whispered the boy. "I am carrying the Heavenly Bread. Please take care of It."

The soldier picked Tarcisius up from the ground and carried him away. He knew that he was carrying not only a dead child, but also the King for whom Tarcisius had died.

He took him back to the priest who carefully took the Blessed Sacrament from under the dead child's cloak.

After that, the body of the martyr was taken away and placed with all the others who had died for their faith.

A Gift from Heaven

All day long, the king's soldiers were looking for people who called themselves Christians. Those that were found were punished. Then the cruel judge would try to make them say there was no God. If they would not do this, they were punished again and then killed.

Now, it happened that a lovely young girl named Dorothy was brought before the judge. When he saw how beautiful she was, he wanted her for a wife. He did everything in his power to save her from death.

"Surely a lady as beautiful as you are should not die so young," he told her.

Dorothy only smiled and said, "I am not afraid to die, for then I shall see Him Whom I love."

"What is the name of the one you love?" the judge asked.

Dorothy answered, "He is Jesus Christ, the Son of the true God."

"Where does this Christ live?" the judge asked.

"As God, He is everywhere," replied the young girl. "His home is in heaven, and it is there that He is waiting for me."

"What nonsense!" laughed the judge. "How can you believe anything like that? There can't be any place more beautiful than the world in which we now live. Think of all of our lovely flowers and plants! Think of the songs of the birds! This is where I want to live forever."

"Oh, but in heaven everything is far more beautiful than it is in this world," said Dorothy softly. "There the flowers never die. There the woods are always green. In heaven, there is no sadness, no sickness, no death."

"Ha! Ha! Ha!" laughed the judge in a loud, cruel voice. He did not believe there could be such a wonderful place.

"If what you claim is true," he said, "I hope you will be good enough to send me something from that wonderful place you call heaven."

That day Dorothy was put to death.

In the evening, the judge had dinner with some of his friends. He told them about Dorothy and the things she had said about heaven.

Then the men laughed and made fun of the Christians. As they were laughing, something happened, and they all became very quiet. They were too frightened to speak.

A little child, dressed in shining white, walked into the room. In his hands, he carried three golden apples and three golden roses.

"These are gifts which Dorothy has sent to you from heaven," the child told the judge.

Then all at once the child was gone.

Now the judge knew that what Dorothy had told him was true. He had learned a great lesson from her.

The very next day, he went to the king and said, "I believe that there is only one true God, and that is the God of the Christians. I am going to be a faithful Christian."

The judge was put to death. In a short time, he was with Dorothy in that happy place called heaven.

Hubert the Hunter

It was a bright spring morning many years ago when Hubert opened his eyes in the palace of the king. "What a wonderful day for hunting," he thought as he looked at the sun coming up over the hills.

There was only one thing that Hubert loved more than hunting, and that was to be with his beautiful wife.

Near the palace where Hubert lived with the king, there were large forests filled with deer. The king's men could go hunting anytime they wanted.

On this day, Hubert dressed quickly. Then he took his hunting horn down from the wall and got ready to leave with his friends.

As he moved about, Hubert's wife heard him and asked, "Where are you going so early in the morning, my lord?"

"To the hunt, my good lady," answered Hubert as he smiled at his wife.

"Today, Hubert?" asked his wife in surprise, as she looked at the crucifix in the room.

"And why not?" asked Hubert.

"This is Good Friday," replied the kind lady. "It is a day for prayer and fasting, not for fun and a good time."

Hubert put his head back and laughed. "You don't suppose the deer in the forest know that it is Good Friday, do you?" he asked.

Hubert's wife looked at him and replied in a soft, gentle voice, "No, Hubert, the deer in the forest do not know what a holy day this is, but we do. We know that Christ died for us. We know that this is the day on which to remember His death and great love for us."

Hubert took his wife's hand in his. "Don't worry about me, my lady," he said. "You can pray and fast and keep the holy day, but I'm off to the hunt."

Many friends joined Hubert in front of the palace gate. The hunters blew their horns. The dogs rushed into the forest, and the hunt began.

After some time, Hubert found himself alone. This was really nothing new for him. It had happened before, and so he thought his dogs would lead him on as they had always done in the past.

But today the forest seemed different. There was a strange stillness in the forest and in the valley below. Not even the leaves on the trees were moving. The hunting dogs had never before been so quiet.

Suddenly Hubert saw a large stag down in the valley below him. He turned his horse and started after the stag.

As he came near the valley, his horse stopped running. The horse moved slowly and quietly.

Just then, a wonderfully strange thing happened. The stag turned around and looked at Hubert. The hunter's heart beat fast. He felt frightened, for there between the horns of the stag was a crucifix.

A voice called out, "Hubert, go back to the Lord."

At once, Hubert got off his horse and knelt down on the ground.

"Lord, tell me what to do," prayed Hubert, who now felt very much ashamed of himself.

The voice answered, "Go to My bishop. He will tell you what you must do to save yourself."

Hubert obeyed the voice. He went at once to find the bishop.

After that Good Friday, on which Hubert heard the Lord's voice, he never went hunting. Hubert prayed and fasted all the rest of his life. He lived such a holy life that he became a great saint. We now call him Saint Hubert the hunter.

The Little Hermit

Even when Saint Catherine was only a young girl, she had heard about and thought about hermits. She knew that they lived in caves so they could pray and think about God all the time.

"That would be an easy way to become a saint," she thought to herself. "I think I, too, shall become a hermit. I'll keep it a secret. No one but God will know what I am going to do."

One morning, Catherine got up before the rest of the family. She dressed quickly and went down to the kitchen. There she got a small loaf of bread and some water.

Then out of the house and through the yard she ran until she reached the road. The sun was coming up over the hills. Flocks of birds were singing, and the sky was getting blue.

"What a nice day this is to go looking for a cave!" the little girl said to herself as she walked along.

Then she began to wonder if perhaps her parents would miss her and send soldiers out to look for her.

"Oh, dear, I hope they won't," she thought. "I can never become a saint in our house. There are too many people around all the time, and there is too much noise. How can anyone think about God in a place with so much noise?"

Just then Catherine saw something that made her cry out with joy. Right in front of her was a hill with a small cave in the side of it.

"Oh, there is my cave!" she cried joyfully as she ran toward a hole in the hill. "Thank You, dear God, for helping me find it so quickly."

The dim cave was not very large, but it was big enough for a very young girl to stand up in.

"I'll stay here all the rest of my life. I'll pray and become holy like the other hermits have done," Catherine said as she walked inside.

Catherine ate a small piece of bread and took a drink of water. Then she knelt down and began to pray.

While she was praying, something very strange happened. Someone spoke to her and said, "Catherine, do you really love Me?"

The voice was kind and gentle. It did not frighten the little girl. She looked around to see where it came from.

"It must be Our Lord," she thought, and she answered with joy, "Yes, Lord, I love You. I would love You more if I could see You."

Then the kind voice spoke again and said, "You want to be a hermit, don't you?"

"Oh, yes," replied the child. "Then I can love You and think about You all the time."

"If you really love Me, you will do what I want, won't you," said the voice.

Catherine answered, "For You, dear Lord, I will do anything. I will even die for You."

"Then go back to your home," said the voice. "Go back to your parents and sisters and brothers. I want some people to be hermits, but not little girls like you."

Catherine was surprised and said, "Oh, I want to be a saint, dear Lord. I can't be one at our house. There are too many people and too much noise."

The gentle voice replied, "Oh, yes, you can, little one. You can become a saint anywhere if you really want to be one. I want you to stay at home. There you can help other people to know and love Me."

"All right," said Catherine as she picked up her little water jar and loaf of bread. "Oh, please, dear Lord, don't let my parents be cross about my coming here, will You?"

The voice did not answer.

Almost before the little girl knew it, she was in front of her own home again. When Catherine's brother John saw her, he ran to meet her. He thought that she had gone to visit their oldest sister who lived near them.

"Why didn't you take me along?" he said to Catherine. "It was mean of you to go to our sister's house without telling me."

"I didn't go there," Catherine replied. "I went away to live in a cave and be a hermit."

"Oh, nonsense!" laughed her brother. "That's just another one of your silly stories. Girls always think of such silly things!" Then the two children ran into the house for lunch.

Catherine lived at home for many years after that. She did as God wanted, and each day she became holier.

Today, Catherine is a great saint in heaven. Her feast comes in the month of April.

Flowers from Heaven

Little Princess Elizabeth lived in a country far across the sea.

When she was only four years old, she had to leave her parents and her home. She had to leave her own country where her father was king and her mother was queen. She had to go to another country to live with the family of a prince. She was to marry the prince some day, when she grew up to be a young lady.

Elizabeth felt excited about the long trip to another country, but her good parents were sad. They did everything they could so that their daughter would be happy while she was away from home.

One spring day, some servants took little Princess Elizabeth to another palace where she was to live until she married the prince.

Little Louis, for that was the name of the prince, was very happy to see the lovely princess he would marry some day. His mother took good care of the two children and taught them how to become a good king and queen when they grew up.

The little prince and princess went to school right in the palace. After a few months, they learned to read and to write.

As Princess Elizabeth grew older, she began to read books about Our Lord and the saints and martyrs.

But Louis' mother did not like to see Elizabeth read these books. She did not care much about God. She thought there were other things more important for a queen to know.

One holy day, Louis' mother took the two children to church. She told them to put on their best clothes and to wear their golden crowns.

When they got to the church, the children saw many other young princes and princesses with shining crowns on their heads.

Prince Louis' mother took the two children to the front seats. There she sat, very proud and straight, between them.

As soon as the Mass began, Elizabeth took the crown off her head and knelt down. It made the prince's mother very angry to see young Elizabeth without her crown and on her knees.

"Elizabeth, what do you mean?" she whispered. "Kings and queens never get down on their knees in church. They are too great for that. Now put on your crown, and sit in your seat."

"I'm sorry," replied the little princess, "but I would be ashamed to do that. Our Lord, the King of heaven and earth, is here on the altar, and He is much greater than we are."

Louis' mother was not pleased to hear Elizabeth say that. Her face became very red. She sat straighter than ever in her seat.

After Elizabeth and Louis grew up, they had a very beautiful wedding and became king and queen of the country.

Every morning, Queen Elizabeth got up early and went to Mass. Then she left the palace and spent the day taking care of the poor and sick in the town.

Now, it happened that Louis' mother was still living in the palace. She thought the young queen was too holy. She used to watch to see if she could catch her doing something wrong.

One year, many of the people in the country had no food to eat, but in King Louis' palace, there was a lot of food.

Elizabeth did not like to think of people being hungry. She wished to share what she had with them. So one morning, the young queen took a loaf of bread from the palace to share with a poor family that she planned to visit that day.

Elizabeth was just leaving the palace when she saw King Louis and his mother. Quickly the young queen tried to hide the bread under her cloak.

"Oh, dear Lord," the queen prayed, "please don't let them see what I have. If they do, the poor family in the village won't have anything to eat today."

The king's mother turned toward her son Louis and said, "I am sure that your wife is carrying off bread from your palace."

The king smiled at his pretty young wife when she came closer. He loved her very much. "What do you have, Elizabeth?" he asked in a gentle voice.

The poor queen was too frightened to speak. She just stood still and held the cloak around her.

Then Louis' angry mother tried to pull open the queen's cloak. As she did so, one large red rose after another fell to the ground.

King Louis and his mother could hardly believe their eyes when they saw the beautiful roses. It was winter, and they knew that roses could not grow in ice and cold weather.

After that day, King Louis loved his wife more than ever. He knew that Our Lord had helped Elizabeth because she was so good to His poor.

Elizabeth is now a great saint in heaven. Many little girls receive her name when they are baptized. Melissa Lake took it for her Confirmation name.

The Little Flower of Jesus

Therese Martin, who is now one of our great saints, lived many years ago with her large family. Her family took good care of her, just as your family takes good care of you.

As a child, Therese did many of the same things that other children like to do. She liked to play with her toys and to play games with other children. She liked to draw pretty pictures. She loved pretty clothes and was always happy to wear them.

There was one thing Therese liked to do best of all. That was to go fishing with her father and carry her lunch in a basket. Often she sat on the ground beside him and played that she was catching fish in her little net. She also liked to watch the flocks of birds as they flew high over her head.

Sometimes the little girl grew tired of being quiet while her father was fishing. Then she would run about and play in the woods or pick flowers for her altar at home. She loved every flower and everything that God made.

Little Therese wanted very much to become a saint, but she was only a small child. She knew she could not do hard things like the martyrs and some of the great saints had done. She asked Our Lord to show her a way, and He did.

Therese called it "The Little Way." She gave it that name because it is for anyone who wants to become a saint.

This is how Therese became a saint. When she was given something to eat that she did not like, she ate it. She never let anyone know she didn't like it.

When she was told to wear a dress that she did not want to wear, she put it on anyway. She tried to be happy about it.

Sometimes when she wanted to go out and play, she was told to help with the housework or to do her school work. Therese obeyed with a smile on her face.

Therese learned to smile when she felt cross. She learned to say only kind words, and never words that would hurt others.

She learned to be kind and good, even to boys and girls who were unkind to her. She often shared her toys and candy with them.

These are not always easy things to do, but they became easy for Therese because she offered them all to Jesus. It is easy to do hard things for someone you love, and Therese loved Our Lord very, very much.

That is the way Therese learned to become a saint. She did the everyday things in the very best way she could. Then she offered them to Jesus with her love.

Therese wanted to be a missionary, but she could not. So she became a helper by offering her prayers for those in far-away missions.

When Therese Martin grew older, she became a nun. She asked to be named Sister Therese of the Child Jesus.

She was a nun for only a few years before she became ill and died.

Just before the holy nun left this world, she made a promise. She said that when she got to heaven, she would send roses down into this world.

She did not mean real roses that grow on plants. God's flowers in heaven are the blessings that each one of us receives.

Little Saint Therese loved and served God so well that He now sends us the blessings she asks for us. Her roses are the answers to our prayers.

People call Saint Therese the "Little Flower of Jesus" because she loved God's flowers that grew here on earth and she loves God's flowers in heaven.

Confirmation Time Comes

As the time for Confirmation grew nearer, the boys and girls thought about the new names they would take.

Peggy took the name Therese because she liked the Little Flower's way of becoming a saint. "I cannot do hard things, but I can do little things and offer them to God as Saint Therese did," she told her mother.

Melissa thought she would like to be named Elizabeth. Melissa liked Saint Elizabeth because she was so good and shared things with the poor. Matt took Francis for his Confirmation name. He liked the kind saint who gave up all his riches to become poor like Our Lord.

Peter felt that Saint Peter was one of the greatest saints in heaven, and so he wanted to keep that name for his Confirmation name, too.

The children had learned in class that when they were baptized they had been made the children of God. Now, through Confirmation, they were all to become stronger in their love for God.

In this new sacrament, God would send His Holy Spirit upon them, just as He had once sent the Holy Spirit upon the apostles.

When they received the Holy Spirit, It would help them in a special way to love God and give them the power to become stronger Christians.

One evening in the month of May, the bishop came to Timber Town once again. This time he had come to confirm the children and grownups who were ready to be made strong in their love for God.

As he turned toward them, the bishop prayed, "May the Holy Spirit come down upon you, and the power of the Most High keep you from all sin."

The children and grownups answered, "Amen."

Then after a while, they walked up to the altar where the bishop confirmed each one alone.

Matt and Peter were there. Peggy and Melissa were there with many other boys and girls.

They were happy they had received the sacrament which marked them as special members of God's great family.

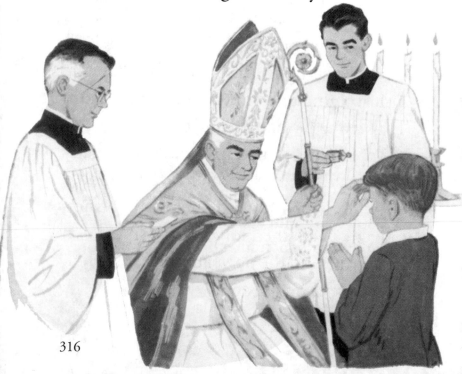

Within My Soul

I am so glad to be alive,
To run and play and grow;
There are so many things to do
There is so much to know.

Inside me is a secret life,
Hidden where I can't see;
For, deep within my soul, lives God—
The Blessed Trinity.

E.S.

To the Teacher

This Is Our Town, Revised Edition, is the Initial Third Reader of the FAITH AND FREEDOM Basic Readers. It is designed to provide growth in the basic reading skills for children in the first half of the third grade. This text intro-duces 350 new words, 299 of which (starred in the list below) can be recognized independently by the pupil through the application of various word-attack skills developed in the manuals of the preceding books of the series and reviewed in the manual accompanying this text.

The content of this initial third reader emphasizes the theme of Christian solidarity in man's civic and social life. Stories illustrate that this solidarity is made possible only when individuals are conscious of their relationship to one another because of their common sonship in the same Heavenly Father and their common brotherhood in Christ.

WORD LIST

UNIT I
7. Timber*
   airport*
----
8. flight*
   St.*
9. Matt*
10. serve*
11. . . .
12. . . .
13. space*
----
14. Mars*
    station
    suits*
15. Marty*
16. field
    river *
    climbed
17. moon*
    rocket*
18. life*
19. . . .
----
20. trouble
    Melissa
21. screamed*
    upstairs*
    ink*

22. rubbed*
    spots*
23. . . .
24. . . .
25. . . .
----
26. (Poem)
----
27. suddenly*
    shrill*
28. whistle
    short*
29. iron
30. chief
    ladder*
    brave*
31. ambulance*
32. parrot*
    cage*
33. . . .
----
34. errands
35. apartment*
    fourth*
    floor*
36. elevator*
    safe*
37. coffee*
38. wonder*

39. . . .
----
40. earns*
    package*
41. . . .
42. watched
    quickly*
43. . . .
44. whisper*

UNIT II
45. forest*
    Indians*
----
46. toward
    Yohocan*
    visit*
47. canoe
48. tied*
    themselves*
49. hour*
    rope*
50. village*
51. shouted*
52. Sacrament*
53. true*
54. . . .
55. end*

56. baptize*
    women
57. set*
----
58. Buffalo*
    hunt*
    winter*
59. kill*
    skin*
    scolded*
60. felt*
    bow*
    arrows*
61. strong*
    shiny*
    enemy *
62. believe
    angry*
    knife*
63. . . .
64. boasted*
    camp*
65. held*
----
66. spring*
67. crucifix*
68. fighting*
    wigwams*
69. Blackrobe*

318

70. . . .
71. belongs*
    squaw*
72. sugar
    Cloud*
73. promise
74. below*
    greeted*
75. brought*
76. . . .
----
77. earth*
78. path*
    bushes
    scratches*
79. . . .
80. . . .
81. pointed*
    snake*
82. . . .
----
83. (Poem)
----
84. early*
85. lay*
    peddler*
86. trade*
    corn*
87. . . .
88. months
89. hiding*
90. strike*

UNIT III
91. . . .
92. Prince*
    flooded*
    closed*
93. replied*
    weather*
94. bicycle*
    hope*
95. floating*
    log*
96. . . .
97. sand*
    buildings
    behind*
----
98. speed*
    born*

99. sea*
    rowing*
    Charlie*
100. across*
101. . . .
102. . . .
103. . . .
----
104. park* cave*
105. dangerous*
    wild*
    zoo*
106. listen
    growl*
107. won't*
    alive*
108. high
    flashlight*
    corner*
109. puppy*
110. . . .
111. spoke*
112. fed*
----
113. . . .
114. kitchen*
    planned*
    maple*
115. wrote*
    worry
    closet*
116. send*
117. syrup*
118. harm*
    cost*
    dollar*
----
119. west*
120. . . .
121. shaking*
122. theater
123. sacrifice*
    sins*
    knelt*
124. already *
----
125. special
    March*
    bishop*
126. sewing

    cloths*
127. past*
    join*
128. stand*
129. . . .
----
130. (Poem)

UNIT IV
131. tale*

132, scrap*
133. strings*
134. wide*
    ruffle*
    bottom*
135. wet*
    finger*
136. easy *
----
137. inventor*
    machines
    rich*
138. front*
    stilts*
    caught*
139. swatter
    breeze*
    cool*
140. sails *
    grass*
    fence*
141. rid*
----
142. often*
143. . . .
144. dust*
145. rolls
    bake*
146. flat*
    forgotten*
    yeast*
147. . . .
148. sweet*
----
149. Buffy*
    Tuffy*
    Stuffy*
150. flour*
    fluffy*

    puffy*
151. . . .
152. . . .
153. oven*
    added*
154. . . .
155. . . .
----
156. brass*
    young
    worth*
157. clever*
    afraid*
158. nonsense*
159. greedy *
160. dumplings*
161.
162. luck*
163. . . .
164. . . .
----
165. fiddle*
    penny*
166. counted*
167. . . .
168. . . .
169. . . .
170. important*
171. shop*
172. . . .
173. tore*
174, leading*
175. . . .
----
176. (Poem)

UNIT V
177. orchestra
    programs
----
178. member*
    idea
179. porch*
180. Frank*
    twenty-five*
    chocolate*
181. flutes*
    tune*
182. pushed

183. allowed*
184. . . .
185. . . .
186. during
187. . . .
188. Haydn
     cousin
     market*
189. violin*
     perhaps*
190. else
191. drum*
     ill*
192. low*
     Mt*
193. . . .
194. . . .
195. . . .
----
196. concert*
     manners*
     meals*
197. gasped*
198. taste*
199. terrible
     raised*
200. . . .
201. kept*
----
202. (Poem)
----
203. summer*
     treasured
204. . . .
205. . . .
206. passed*
207. crowd*
208. death*
     amen*
209. . . .
----
210. Jenny*
     nightingale*
     Lind*
211. lessons*
212. blackberry*
     America*
213. Fails*
     lot*
214. daughter*
215. wren's*
     secret*

216. favor*
217. . . .
218. . . .

219.
        Rumpel-
        stiltskin*
        servant*
        miller's*
220. lazy*
     spins*
     straw*
221. pile*
     majesty*
222. knees*
223. mind*
224. heart
225. . . .
226. . . .
227. brewing*
     claim*
228. witch*

        UNIT VI
229. citizens*
     April*
----
230. wolf
     picnic*
231. . . .
232. tame*
233. gentle*
     rushing*
     straight*
234. soft*
235. . . .
236. . . .
237. . . .
238. roast*
     hurrah*
----
239. committee*
240. . . .
241. whined*
     explained*
242. . . .
243. . . .
244. finally*
245. neck*
246. . . .
247. . . .

248. . . .
----
249. paved*
     muddy*
     dry*
250. class*
251. . . .
252. ashamed*
253. mine*
254. . . .
255. flocked*
----
256. . . .
257. straps*
     Louis
258. . . .
259. spent*
260. . . .
261. . . .
262. yesterday'
----
263. stripes*
264. . . .
265. suppose*
     state*
     thirteen*
266. . . .
267. . . .
268. . . .
269. . . .
270. saluted*
271. . . .
----
272. (Poem)

        UNIT VII
273. Confirma-
        tion
----
274. Christians
     dimly*
275. faith*
     Tarcisius
     refuse*
276. . . .
277. . . .
278. whom*
279. such*
280. cruel*
     beat*
     dead*

281. martyr
----
282. judge*
     Dorothy
     power*
283. . . .
284. . . .
285. . . .
286. . . .
287. Hubert*
     deer*
288. . . .
289. . . .
290. valley*
     stag*
291. . . .
292. . . .
----
293. hermit*
     Catherine
     loaf*
294. noise*
295. joy*
296. . . .
297. . . .
298. . . .
299. . . .
----
300. Elizabeth
     marry
301. . . .
302. seat*
303. . . .
304. share*
305. . . .
306. . . .
307. . . .
----
308. Therese
309. . . .
310. . . .
311. . . .
312. nun*
313. . . .
----
314. . . .
315. Spirit*
316. . . .
----
317. (Poem)

ABCDEFGHIJK 06987654 3

PRINTED IN THE UNITED STATES OF AMERICA

9863—F. & F.: This is Our Town, Rev.

Printed in the USA
CPSIA information can be obtained
at www.ICGtesting.com
CBHW051438291024
16558CB00003B/206